LOOKING FOR HAPPINESS IN ALL THE WRONG PLACES

Holly Heald

Holly Heald
www.lookingfor.life

Book Layout © 2017 BookDesignTemplates.com

Looking for Happiness in All the Wrong Places Holly Heald. -- 1st ed.
ISBN 978-1-8381974-0-7

Dedicated to John Andrews
(1950 – 2008)

CONTENTS

MOMENTS IN TIME

How many of us have experienced moments in our lives when we suddenly understand something that's eluded us for years? In just seconds the answer seems so obvious it could be emblazoned across the sky; yet moments before it seemed impossible.

This book is the culmination of three such 'moments' in my life; moments which have marked and changed me forever.

It was Eurovision night. We had spent the evening watching the amusing spectacle of Europe's vocal and musical talents; helped by the dry wit of the much loved and now departed broadcaster Terry Wogan. The outlook for the British entry was unpromising and we were reaching for the remote control.

A telephone call interrupted our dilemma. My dad had collapsed. Unswayed by Eurovision he had been watching Victor Meldrew's last moments on the infamous BBC television series "One Foot in the Grave". One of his favourite programmes we often joked that he was becoming like Victor. I listened as my sister described the paramedics' attempts to revive him, and eventually, their decision to stop; as thousands mourned the loss of a television hero, my dad died.

Speeding to my parent's house, distracted by the traffic which slowed our progress I had not prepared myself for the enormity of death. I would have added certain complexity to the autopsy that would follow without the quick response of the paramedics, who stopped the door slamming into his head as I rushed into the lounge - his body was lying somewhere between the sofa and the door, his face cruelly contorted as if he were the victim of a heinous crime; the result of the attempts to revive him I later learnt.

My dad was in his fifties and I know that he was more fortunate than so many others; yet his death changed me in a way I did not expect. Beyond the grief that painfully and rudely gripped my body I had been reminded of our mortality; the certainty that we would all die. But, most of all I had been reminded that life can be too short for putting off the things that are really important to us. I realised that I had rather fancifully imagined that I would be warned if my life were to end; and during that time, I would find sudden and unimaginable motivation to do the things I always meant to - but somehow never got around to. But my dad had no warning - his life was snuffed out like an electric light in a power cut. I realised that my priorities were often muddled; the things that really mattered to me were not the things I devoted most of my spare time to; I realised that if I was not careful, not so many years later, my life too would end and my dreams would end with it; unexplored, hidden in the depths of my subconscious.

My thoughts should not have surprised me; for some time I had nurtured a sense that I was not living as my priorities should have dictated. I was slowly realising that I did not want the same things from my life that the world was telling me I should. Instead of being excited by the prospect of living in a wealthier society than ever before I felt sad. Our increasingly materialistic society did not sit comfortably with my values. I hated the thought that whilst I pursued happiness in all things consumable, other people were dying in the thousands and our planet was suffocating under the strain.

My dad cared about these things. In the moments after his death I realised that I could no longer allow the world to carry me on in a whirlwind of work, leisure and selfish and ill-informed pursuit of my own pleasure. I felt challenged to break the mould, to explore how my life could be different.

To an observer, the second moment was unremarkable. I was comfortably nestled in my favourite armchair reading a book. Yet the authors' haunting account of his experience at a refugee camp in Ethiopia deeply affected me as he recounted watching a young boy die from malnutrition. Two years old, a similar age to my eldest daughter at that time, he depicted a slow and painful death as the boy died just a few yards from his own family who were too ill to notice. As I read part of me wanted to scream, "why didn't you do something?", my imagination taking me to a world of emergency services, ambulances and doctors battling to save his life. But there were little resources and nothing anybody could do except watch the little boy die; an image the author can never forget.

I was sickened by his words but not surprised; the world is wrought with poverty. Whilst many of us have more than we could ever need, billions of people are living without enough food to nourish them or water to quench their thirst. Whilst I worry about what I am going to wear each morning millions of people wear the same clothes day in, day out. There is desperate poverty in even the richest countries; severe hardship may be just a few doors away yet we carry on regardless.

I was crushed by the realisation that although I cared about other people and value fairness, I was still content to consume more than my fair share of the world's resources. My actions were not deliberate. It was simply too easy to compete for material success without thinking about the consequences. I was happy to make money, and then make it go as far as possible so I can get the things I wanted (despite reassuring myself that I really needed them). I didn't like the thought that I was buying my clothes from retailers that take advantage of the poor – but what alternatives did I have. I didn't like to think that families were starving to death whilst I throw away food that has gone off. I didn't like the thought that my mindless and sometimes greedy consumption of the world's natural resources may deprive entire generations – perhaps my own children – of things we take for granted today, but what choice did I have. As I contemplated the terrible death suffered by the child in this harrowing account, I understood that I could no longer pursue my own ambitions in life without doing something.

The third moment was the least dramatic yet the most defining. Desperate to escape December's driving rain and with over an hour to wait for a train home, I had sought refuge in a Wine Bar in Taunton, UK pondering - of all things - economics. In the final throws of a business and economics degree I was wondering how many people really understand the main economic concepts on which we build our world - namely economic growth - and from which stems our understanding of the world, and our role in it. It seems only sensible that if we are to devote our lives to the pursuit of economic growth, we understand what it is; that our role is not purely by chance or apathy. In fact, to participate in the race for economic growth without understanding what it is or how it works seems foolhardy, stupid even.

In that moment I realised that this is exactly how we are conditioned to behave. Rather than rational, enlightened members of our economies working towards our goals we live in the world like actors in a play who have learnt our lines but do not know the plot. From the moment we are born we join a treadmill of education, training and work, for most a daily toil to earn enough money to live; always striving for more, our success judged by the things we acquire; our country's success judged by its economic achievements; and we do not stop to ask why.

Reflecting on my own experience, I realised too that despite the inevitable flaws of being human most people mean well. I cannot believe that deep down we are really comfortable that we struggle with our weight when children and babies are starving to death. I cannot accept that we really like the constant battle against clutter and waste characteristic of modern consumer life. I cannot believe that we really like the thought that our mindless consumption of the world's resources may deprive entire generations of things we take for granted today.

In that moment I realised how easy it is to be an 'actor'; to accept our world as it is regardless of how well it works. Even if we do long for things to be different, we feel that the challenges we face are too big; that we have no choice but to accept things as they are. We forget that we have a capacity for change, and to change things around us. We forget that many of the economic systems and rules we live by are 'man-made' creations intended to make life easier for us; to help make the job of producing and distributing adequate food, water and shelter for us to live comfortably on our planet more efficient.

In these moments I realised that in my forgetfulness, my inertia, and my unwillingness to change I had adopted a lifestyle which fed the minority leaving the majority hungry; a lifestyle which distributed resources away from the people who need them most to those who already have more than they can appreciate; a lifestyle which was destroying our natural environment at an alarming rate; a lifestyle which condemned animals to lives of misery; and not least, despite an unwavering belief that it was good for me, a lifestyle that was not contributing to my wellbeing. Because, although we are living at a time when many of us have more than ever before there is little evidence to suggest that we are any happier. In fact, many studies suggest that levels of happiness and wellbeing are at similar or even lower levels than in the past.

Could it be that we are compromising all that is important to us in an ill-fated pursuit of happiness?

CHAPTER ONE

IN PURSUIT OF HAPPINESS

There's no doubt that time passes more slowly the more impatient we are. I was wondering why I couldn't get used to this simple fact as I stared at the kettle willing it to boil so that I could return to my daughter with a much-needed cup of coffee. The morning had certainly been trying; meetings to cancel, a doctor's appointment to arrange – never easy at eight a.m., one child to get to school and another, her face as pale as the milk I was willing her to drink; a fever indicating what she was too young to say, she wasn't well.

That's why I was determined not to leave the room unarmed. Yet I had a nagging feeling I should. As I watched the steam rise from the now almost boiling water the nagging feeling became a persistent urge. Sighing I turned away from certain enjoyment and hastened to the lounge. And thank goodness I did. My daughter's skin was no longer pale but a greyish blue. Her body was rigid as steel but her limbs were flailing about like a palm tree in a tornado threatening to topple her precious body from the worn brown leather of our sofa and onto the unforgiving wooden floor.

How I reached her in time I will never know but moments later I laid her convulsing body on the floor and watched in horror as foam poured from her mouth as if it had been filled with fairy liquid. Dialling 999 is difficult when in shock. Harder still when the buttons on your mobile phone are so small they would be more appropriate for a child's toy. After several attempts I discarded my phone in disgust running for the landline in the hall.

As her complexion became a starker blue the emergency operator began to explain the resuscitation procedure. I frantically tried to recall my first aid training – if my suspicions were correct, I doubted the lesson I had at Girl Guides decades earlier would suffice. I was praying for Divine intervention when she took a sudden breath; apparently not uncommon in her condition. Soon after the paramedic arrived, muttered a few words, rushed back to his vehicle and returned with a confusing array of equipment. Shortly my baby girls' limbs stilled and she was whisked into a waiting ambulance.

I had often imagined what it would be like to be in an ambulance with its flashing blue lights and sirens blaring, announcing our important journey to the world. I had given it an almost fantastical quality. I hadn't imagined it would be like this. My life was falling apart. One of the most precious things in the World to me was lying helpless in an ambulance. Not permitted to sit with her all I could do was watch – it could have been the length of a football pitch from where she lay to my seat - and pray. At that moment I would have given anything, everything to know that she would be well again. Nothing was more important.

The rest of the story became history as I watched her two years later, confident and beautiful practicing her all important role as a camel for her first school nativity play. As she complained that the eye holes, I cut her in her camel mask were too small; her blonde hair catching the light against the woollen camel hair I thought about the hours that passed that day in hospital. By arrival her vitals had stabilized, and, transferred to A&E's resuscitation area she was dubbed Sleeping Beauty by the doctors who examined her as hour by hour she lay perfectly still, her complexion once again pale and her temperature returning to normal.

A double ear infection turned out to be the culprit; far less frightening than the possibilities I had imagined. But anyone who has witnessed a febrile convulsion will tell you how scary it is. With little reassurance to the contrary moments passed in that ambulance when I thought she may die.

Reflecting on that experience, I am reminded how easy it is to understand our values when faced with the question of life and death, and how easy it is to forget them in the business of everyday life. No-one watches Titanic and wonders why people couldn't buy themselves a ticket on one of the few lifeboats. It's obvious that faced with the question of death, money has little meaning. In the same way I would have given everything I had for my daughter to be well.

Yet, at the often hectic pace of modern life it is easy to forget the bigger picture. Rather than working towards the things that are really important, we get side-tracked in the pursuit of things we mistakenly think are important to us.

When I was a little girl in the months leading up to Christmas, I spent hours flicking through the Argos catalogue, dreaming of what Father Christmas may bring, and then later of what I may be able to persuade my parents to buy me. I suppose for many of us that's where our love affair with toys, and gadgets, games and music systems, mobile phones – you name it - starts. One year I truly believed that if I could just have that television my life would be complete. It seems silly now; ridiculous even. The black and white television I coveted had a hazy reception and it was difficult to tune the channels. Yet I truly believed it would make me happy. I smile as I recall the time it nearly set the house on fire. A fact I kept from my parents for years. Now I realise that I thought the same of so many of the things I dedicated my life to. It seems impossible that I missed important family occasions because I was busy at work. Somehow, I thought it was more important to work than celebrate my dad's birthday. I wish I could tell him now how sorry I am that I turned up so late. Sadly, the opportunity has passed now.

Amongst the origins of rules like 'thou shall not murder' and 'thou shall not steal' sits the tenth commandment; "thou shall not covet". Yet whilst murder and theft remain outlawed with severe consequences for those guilty of these crimes, to covet has undergone a radical transformation; now forming the very foundation of modern society. We are rarely encouraged to reflect on our emotional or spiritual needs, but we are often encouraged to covet. In fact, we need to covet to be good consumers. Modern organisations go a step further and create needs for us – things we did not even realise we need. Clever marketing campaigns convince us that going without these essentials would make life unbearable. Who would have thought that the birth of your first child necessitates a people carrier or four by four, or that we must wear a different outfit for every special occasion? It is so easy to get caught up in this way of thinking and before long we start to believe that we can't cope without, or we'll be ridiculed. I've recently served as the President for the local institute of my professional body. Alongside less glamorous responsibilities I was privileged to attend a number of black-tie dinners across the UK. Inspired by accounts of famous people 'hiring' outfits to reduce waste whilst still looking fabulous, I didn't want to buy a new dress for each occasion. However, I was haunted by a childhood memory when at the tender age of thirteen I was publicly mocked for wearing the same outfit to a disco I'd worn at a recent party. The humiliation could have been yesterday. Eventually I brought a new dress and a pair of sparkly shoes to replace a pair I had broken a few months before at an awards dinner in London; miraculously I hadn't fallen over as I climbed onstage to accept an award. Over my 'presidency' I wore through every possible combination in my wardrobe, marvelling at how easy it would have been to hit the shops. I wonder how many people have countless outfits and shoes they rarely wear. I guess I should be grateful no tabloids were waiting to write something horrible about me or put a nasty picture on social media to humiliate me in the same way I had been years before.

Yet our culture continues to dictate what we should consume; the latest mobile phone, new cars, trendy sofas and luxury services. In fact, it is hard to go anywhere without being subject to the allure of advertisement campaigns — claiming to be the answer to our heart's desires. Even our children innocently participate, nagging us to buy them the latest toy or a popular snack for their lunch box. I particularly dislike the trend for 'fake food; arguing with my daughter that it may be her 'favourite' but cheese really isn't supposed to be elastic and that you are supposed to eat it and not play with it. Clever branding tells us that products are capable of delivering more than the product itself. I think we have probably all had moments when we have been tempted to buy a new tracksuit or pair of trainers, imagining that one purchase will overnight see us transformed from couch potatoes to fit and talented athletes ready to win the Olympics. That somehow, rather than hide under the covers on a cold, dark winter's morning, we will want to leap out of bed and jog a few miles around the block. If we are honest, we know the outcome – we will soon be back under the covers quicker than a flash and our new purchases will be relegated to the bottom drawer. Deep down we do know that products – even great products – cannot actually deliver more than what they physically are. Trainers may make running more comfortable, or easier, but they cannot actually change our attitude. That requires something more.

Of course, it would be dishonest to say that consumerism cannot be fun. We all have our little – or big – things we enjoy. A friend of mine has a weakness for mobile phones. Regardless of how many he owns or how well they work, when a new model becomes available, he wants it.

Consumerism wouldn't be a problem if it was good for us and our world, yet increasing evidence suggests it isn't. Few can deny the damage it inflicts on our environment with troubling consequences for the future; and the fact that whilst a minority enjoy lives of plenty, many more live in abject poverty. But what if it is not doing us much good either?

Living in a world obsessed with consumption can certainly be a tiring affair. One year, like a fool I admitted that I am not a fan of Christmas. Whilst festivities and family time are close to my heart, the by-products are not; I hate the hustle and bustle; the stress; the last minute dash to the shops because I received an unexpected present; the endless demands on my time which somehow should fit into my already busy life. Before I had gained ground on my anti-Christmas tirade, I felt a silence descend around the table where I was enjoying a mid-morning coffee. "You don't like Christmas?" a friend exclaimed shocked her biscuit frozen in mid-air all thoughts of dunking it in her drink forgotten with my terrible confession; "Why ever not?" she demanded. I should have stopped talking. Instead I dealt another blow admitting that I dread receiving presents…not just mine but my children's too – the biscuit remained in mid-air as in full flow I couldn't help myself as I confessed that each year a number of presents head straight to my local charity shop. I know I should be grateful someone has kindly brought one of my daughters another teddy bear. Instead I secretly plan how I can pass the poor bear to my local Oxfam shop while he still looks new without my daughter (or husband) noticing. As for my presents…well firstly I should stress that my nearest and dearest do treat me to gifts which I enjoy and treasure. It is the 'feel like I have to give you a present' gifts that are usually the problem. Too often they seem to be given with little thought or consideration as to what I might like. Perhaps, I wonder, the giver is just another person with too many things to do and too little time to do them, eager to tick the job off an already endless list. We all know the gifts I mean. It's the car cleaning kit when you are addicted to the local car wash, soap collections when soap brings you out in a rash, or the 'lovely ornament' which secretly you hope the children will smash into hundreds of tiny pieces. You may notice that I have not mentioned socks. The thing is that I rather like receiving socks. At least they can be useful, or, if not, can easily be passed onto someone else. However, the gifts I particularly dislike are cheap and almost always tacky, stocking fillers; cheap versions of products that might otherwise be useful; little plastic toys and jewellery, cheap nail varnish and beauty products. Sometimes it is not even clear what they are but you know that they face one of two fates; they will either clutter your home or add to the contribution you make to your local landfill site. Oh, the guilt! These are the things you can't even give away.

Christmas day comes and goes, and aided by a steady supply of drinks it's soon over. Then the Boxing Day sales arrive. One Christmas, nine months and one day into my first pregnancy, we went to the boxing day sales to distract ourselves from impending labour. The shop's brightly lit aisles displayed an array of electrical bargains and we found ourselves in a world of televisions, DVD players and music systems blaring out a mixture of old films and Christmas tunes, each machine vying for attention like a drunk at a karaoke party. Suddenly nauseous I perched me and my sizeable bump on a television stand and observed my fellow shoppers. For one couple, a heated discussion about how much they could spend; for another, their children whining for more and their parents reminding them of the presents the day before. "But you didn't buy them", I heard one little boy exclaim, "Father Christmas' elves made them". What can you say to that?

The truth is that whilst we all like 'stuff' before long the glow of a new purchase or present fades and we start planning the next treat. Consumerism will never quench our insatiable appetites. We use language like 'if only I had more money then I will be happy' or 'when I get that job I will be fulfilled' only for the original desire to be quickly replaced by another. I remember the handbag that was going to change my life; soft black leather, well designed and very trendy, I thought this one addition to my wardrobe would revolutionise my life. What was I thinking? Before long instead of being carefully stored away from sticky fingers and incontinent cats it was tossed into the cupboard with everything else, and certainly no-one ever came running up to me in the street congratulating me for my impeccable taste! However, I fondly remember the traditional Boxing Day walk with my family. My handbag has certainly seen better days but the laughter, smiles and fun of Boxing Day remain vivid memories.

It is easy to covet someone else's income. We tell ourselves that we are as talented or hardworking and wonder why we don't command a similar salary. It may be true but the reality is that we will always find ways to spend more and it will surprise us how quickly we forget how it was going to change our lives. When I look at the income my husband and I have earned over our working lives it strikes me that regardless of how much we earned – there have been times of plenty and times of going without – we have always managed – often without realising how 'well-off' we were. Without doubt our happiness has not gone up and down in line with our income. In fact, there have been times when we had relatively little – for instance, I remember using plastic boxes as substitute tables in the lounge of our first house – which I recall particularly fondly

'Wealth', of course, is very subjective. We may live in a lovely house, drive a nice car, have plenty to eat and drink but consider ourselves 'poor' because we cannot afford an annual holiday abroad. Or perhaps we go out for a meal with friends, always scanning the menu for the cheapest meal, or skimping on tap water and being stingy with the tip when we have thousands in the bank we just don't want to spend.

Putting aside the annoyance of Christmas 'tack' this is why I really find Christmas so difficult – it's because goods and services will never satisfy our deepest needs. Yet we spend weeks or even months in preparation for Christmas compared to the alarmingly little time we can spend with our family and friends. Christmas, if only about presents, will disappoint; if not on the day, then soon afterwards. Worse, lives dedicated to the pursuit of goods and services not only contribute to the destruction of our beautiful world and uphold poverty for millions, they also distract us from the things that are really important to us, our natural gifts and talents; the things we excel at without having to try too hard, the things that make living that bit more exciting, and the things which, when we embrace them, get us out of bed in the morning.

If we're not careful we may die without really having lived at all

I once read somewhere that '…apathy is like a wasting disease, it wastes lives'. If we are not careful, I think consumerism can have a similar effect. Hours spent shopping, watching television or playing endless video games can waste the chance we each have to develop our natural gifts and talents. Who hasn't watched one of the many reality programmes on television today only to wonder what it would be like to sing or dance that well? Maybe we have envied someone's figure, ability or fitness. Or maybe we dream of being great mothers, fathers, grandmothers or grandfathers, doctors or scientists...

I think many of us harbour secret disappointments; disappointments we can't even admit to ourselves. Things we once dreamed we would do but fear as the years pass we have missed our chance. People we dreamed we would become but instead of investing time and effort in our dreams we disappoint ourselves by chasing after the alluring scent of goods and services or indulge ourselves in the distraction of the internet or television or increasingly, our mobile phones.

I don't think I am alone with my dislike of Christmas. I believe that more and more people are questioning whether inundating friends and family with hundreds of cards and gifts is a good way to show that we care about them. I think more and more people are asking themselves whether this is the right way to celebrate at all. And I believe that even more should.

CHAPTER TWO

WALL-E

Despite a city landscape there is an eerie silence, punctuated by a sound which at first you can't identify. Places where thousands of people might be expected to congregate are deserted. It feels unnatural as if you are the only spectator in a massive football stadium. A foul smell fills the air and you wonder if life is extinct.

The sound grows louder, and, to your surprise, a small metallic figure appears; the sun glaring in its reflection blinding you momentarily. Unbelievably, it appears to be tidying up. You now realise that something is indeed terribly wrong; the streets are littered with debris. In fact, rubbish lines every corner. Towers of compounded waste are obscuring what would otherwise be the crisp silhouette of sky scrapers reaching high into the brilliant blue sky. It becomes clear that the little metallic figure and the strange sound are related. It is collecting and compounding the waste it has collected to add to the existing towers.

You've just met "Wall-e"; a small, 21st century robot. He has been abandoned on planet earth - now devoid of all natural life. His job is to clear up the world's waste. It seems an impossible task as years of unending abuse have come at a terrible cost.

This picture may be extreme, but Disney's academy award winner may not be as farfetched as we imagine. The truth is that as we search for happiness and meaning in the goods and services we consume and the lifestyles we enjoy, the story that Wall-e and (for those who have watched the film) his love, Eve portray may paint a more accurate picture of the future than we might like to imagine.

Einstein, when asked what the most powerful force in the universe is, said compound interest. His critics expecting an entirely different answer – perhaps related to the complex interaction of inter-galactic forces in our universe – were puzzled. Yet Einstein was right; compound interest is one of the most powerful influences modern man has ever known; its effects capable of amassing fortunes over time.

Today, there is an even more powerful force at work; a force so powerful that it forms the basis of national policies and defines our lives. Two hundred years ago it hardly existed. Today it determines the distribution of goods and services in the world. It creates. It can destroy. It can determine who lives and who dies. And without change it may turn our planet into a scene from Wall-e. This force is known as economic growth.

If economic growth plays such an important role in our world, surely, we all understand what it is and how it works? After-all to devote our lives to the pursuit of something we don't really understand seems pretty foolish. Yet, I don't think many of us do really understand its influence on our lives. You may be relieved that I cannot offer years of research to support my observation. However, a scan of social media or a chat with your friends and family will usually suffice. From every walk of life, you will find well-educated people forced to confess that they are not really sure what economic growth is. In fact, pressed harder many may be unsure exactly what an economy is, and why it is important. Perhaps that's why as the Covid-19 pandemic spread across the world, people posted ignorant comments on social media. My favourite was "we need to find a way of doing life without an economy".

We recognise that crises like Covid-19, the credit crunch and those that have gone before them are bad news for 'wealth' and may long for the economy to get back on track, but how many of us really understand what we are striving for? Thankfully you do not need an economics degree to get to grips with the basics – this may be a relief to those who would associate studying for a degree in economics with slow torture - and whilst we do not need to become experts, I believe it is essential that we understand the basic principles if we are to make sense of the world as it is today.

Every morning in the depth of my subconscious I become aware of a noise, which gradually intensifies, or, if I have set the alarm too loud, shocks me from sleep. I groan as I remember that it's the morning and time to get up. For a moment I wish that everything in my life would just stop for a while; that rather than get out of bed I could lie back, relax and leave the rest of the world to get on with it. I am sure many share my thoughts. Yet, however tempting, we would soon see the problem for we would have to do something with our lives, or else we would surely starve to death. This simple concept is at the heart of economics. To live we have to work (or at least, most of us do).

Whilst our ancestors spent their days cultivating and tending the land to feed themselves and their families, many of us have become divorced from the land and 'enslaved' to work in hospitals, offices, factories, schools and so on; the amount of money we earn dictating the lifestyles we enjoy. Of course, there are exceptions. Increasingly people are rediscovering their links to the land. In the 1970s the driving force of one of the earliest self-subsistence families in the UK, John Seymour writes "Here we all sit, Sally, my wife, Jane who is five and a half, Ann who is two and a half, and Kate who is seven (days), a mile from a hard road, with no electricity, no gas, no deliveries of anything at all excepting coal, provided that we take at least a ton, and mail, and the post woman who gets specially paid for coming here. And we are self-supporting for every kind of good excepting tea, coffee, flour, sugar and salt. We have no car - we drive about with a pony and cart. If the world blew itself up tomorrow, we could go on living quite happily here and hardly notice the difference[1]". John's book 'The fat of the land' is a delightful and heart-warming tale of his family's pursuit for independence from the modern economy as they develop and farm five acres of land in Suffolk.

Despite growing interest in self-subsistence lifestyles few of us could match John's claims nor, perhaps, should we aim to. As I glance out of my window, I wonder how my family would fare in a disaster. A dreadful suspicion comes over me that we would be amongst the first in line to claim whatever charity were available or face certain starvation. I chuckle morbidly as I wonder how long the few strawberries we grew last summer would nourish us.

It's hardly rocket science that we need to work to earn money to live. Neither is it surprising that we share our planet with billions of other people who also rely on its

---

[1] 'The fat of the land' John Seymour (1961) published by permission of Little Toller Books, Copyright the estate of John Seymour

resources. Although it is not a particularly comfortable thought that around a quarter of us consume three quarters of the world's resources, again, I don't think we would be surprised. We certainly produce a lot of waste to show for it. In the UK the waste we generate in a year is enough to fill the Albert Hall every two hours. The consumption habits of babies alone are shocking. From birth to potty the 'average' baby uses enough nappies to carpet Wembley stadium and Wimbledon's centre court twice over. Since each nappy takes over two hundred years to decompose in landfill, a baby's waste will remain on earth long after its lifetime – even after its body will have decomposed. Still, many of us live our day to day lives with little thought of the resources we consume. It's understandable. I don't really want to be reminded that before I leave my home in the morning, I have consumed more of the world's natural resources than millions of people enjoy in days.

Whatever you believe about creation, I think we would all agree that our planet is extraordinarily clever, capable of supporting billions of lives through intricate and complex ecosystems. But we are being reminded that it has a limit; one which there is now little doubt we are exceeding. Official reports suggest that over half of our ecosystems are either subject to use that is unsustainable or are being damaged. Worse, the majority of the strain is on the ecosystems responsible for the quality of the air we breathe, the water we drink and the food we eat.

When we think about our future, and the future of our children and grandchildren and our friends' children and grandchildren, the only logical conclusion is that we should be aiming to consume less; to preserve and look after our world and protect our future as best we can. But how many of us realise that our current definition of economic success relies on the opposite? Our economies rely on us to consume ever increasing amounts of goods and services to be successful.

That's because we traditionally measure economies by the total amount of goods and services produced within them. For an economy to grow, its total production of goods and services must constantly increase. Who would trust a doctor who advised his overweight patient to gorge on fast food every day? Yet, we trust our governments to protect our futures by consuming more and more of the world's precious resources. It is becoming increasingly important that we understand the reality of this deceptively innocent 'ideal'.

The idea that as consumers we need to consume more and more to make a "success" of our economies has become increasingly familiar. When the 2009 credit crunch induced recession deepened, efforts were made in the UK to encourage us Brits to be "good citizens" and spend, spend, spend in our shops, cities and communities aided by the lowest interest rate Central Banks have ever set with the same medicine initially applied to tackle the Covid-19 pandemic, with potentially dangerous side effects, but that is another story.

However, before we get carried away pointing the finger of blame there is a good explanation for our obsession with economic growth. Despite the usual scepticism it is not because our governments are evil institutions plotting the end of the world. It is because the total amount of goods and services produced in an economy, roughly translates into the amount of money we earn. This means that, in theory, with economic growth we should see an increase in earnings allowing us to consume more and more. Few would be tempted to vote for politicians whose manifesto included a promise to shrink the economy and reduce household income. The amount of money we earn in turn affects the amount of money governments receive as tax to run the country, invest in and develop infrastructure and provide public services. Of course, not all governments can be trusted to do so wisely.

Perhaps the easiest way to think about the benefits of economic growth is to think about the rather more emotive subject of recession. Recession is its opposite. It occurs when, instead of growing, the total amount of goods and services produced in an economy shrinks over a specific period of time - usually two successive quarters of a year. In times of recession profits fall, businesses fail, people lose their jobs, families struggle to keep their heads above water, stockmarkets fall and we bemoan the subsequent reduction in the value of our investments and pensions; times, generally, are 'hard' for many people. Of course, we all define 'hard' differently. For some of us 'hard' may mean that we cannot afford our early morning latte and have to wait until we get to work for our caffeine fix, or perhaps we can only afford to eat out once a month. Many of us fall into this category if we are really honest. For others 'hard' may mean poverty – a genuine lack of food and shelter. It's no secret that the use of food banks has increased significantly in recent years as people struggle to afford life's basics.

The benefits of economic growth are clear; generally, it creates higher average incomes, increasing people's access to goods and services and helping them enjoy higher standards of living. During the Twentieth Century it brought radical change, reduced poverty and increased life expectancy. Living in the UK today it's hard to imagine what life was like without the safety net of benefits provided by modern governments.

Less than a century ago, deaths from infectious diseases were common and often people would die following a relatively short period of illness. I sometimes feel like a cat with nine lives because had I been born fifty years ago, I would have already died twice from child bearing complications.

There are many countries that are still in desperate need of the right type of economic growth as it enables people to escape the worst levels of poverty. Even small levels of growth can facilitate higher living standards and better life expectancy through availability of clean water, improved public services, access to medicine and medical expertise and education. The wrong type of economic growth, however, can bring hardship, increase inequalities and create pollution and congestion.

Many of us will fondly – or otherwise - recall our childhood fears. For many years I was afraid of the dark. Only on the third or fourth time of waking in the night and needing the little girls' room would I force myself to descend the ladder of the bunk bed I shared with my sister, expecting at any moment for something or someone to grab my ankles. From there it was anxious sprint to the bathroom opposite, my heart pounding as my brain conjured up images of the horrors awaiting me. In his book, 'When a Billion Chinese Jump[2]' author, Jonathan Watts, describes his boyhood nightmare; the Chinese. Thanks to his school master Watts believed that the Chinese were so numerous that if they all jumped together the collective force of their descent would knock the world off its axis killing us all.

Today we should be afraid of what the Chinese represent; billions of people joining us in the pursuit of success

---

[2] 'When a Billion Chinese Jump', Jonathan Watts (2010)

in the goods and services we consume. Many researchers agree that consumption will increase several times over in the next 30 years.

You don't need to be a genius to work out that yet more pressure on the earth will be an enormous strain. We are facing the prospect that without serious change our natural habitat could literally disappear. Whilst we busy ourselves with our short-term personal agendas research suggests that we have lost 60% of the earth's plants and animals since the 1970s and current rates of extinction are higher than ever before[3]. Biodiversity is fundamental to the future development of humanity. Yet it is increasingly threatened by the way we use and abuse our natural environment. We may literally be stamping out the cure for cancer or chopping down the tree of life in the name of progress.

Predictions of overpopulation, starvation and death are hardly new. In the seventeenth century clergyman Thomas Malthus predicted that the human race was growing faster than it could produce food. Malthus believed that the world's population would reach a size when it would simply run out of food and billions of people would starve. Thankfully, despite localised poverty, 'doomsday' remains a preserve of films as modern production techniques have exponentially increased food supplies (irrespective of distribution issues - we must not forget that it is a terrible

---

[3] 'Living Planet Report 2018', WWF (2018)

injustice that in areas of the world people are dying from the effects of overeating whilst in others men, women and children are dying of starvation.)

But what do we think about our future? Not only do we need to produce enough to feed a growing population, but as the ranks of middle classes grow, we face the challenge of producing enough meat to cater for our changing dietary demands. According to investment analysts more and more of the world's population have enough money to eat like us and they are. Investors have jumped at the chance to get in on the game as agricultural firms are tipped to provide inflation busting returns. With estimates that over a billion people from China and India will join the ranks of the middle classes over the coming years, the question of how meat supplies will keep pace with demand is a sobering thought. The grain alone required to feed livestock will put an unprecedented strain on agriculture and may leave basics like bread unaffordable for many.

I have always thought it surprising that I reached my thirties without a serious hearing problem. That's because in the early years of my marriage, my husband had the dubious pleasure of being a sound engineer. He would spend his evenings sitting at the back of a darkened, smoke filled room (this was before the days of the smoking ban) trying to create a good mix for what were often deluded 'hopefuls'. The experience could be so tedious that on occasions I would accompany him, to offer moral support; although the prospects of conversation were at best limited as despite his efforts to keep the volume within reasonable levels, musicians would always want more. During these evenings I became very familiar with the concept of feedback. Frequently, band members would venture into the audience resulting in an ear-piercing screech as tiny ambient noises would be picked up by the 'hopefuls'' microphones and amplified by their loudspeakers over and over again until the noise was deafening. We need to understand that today's predictions about our future make no account for the increasing speed at which we may see our environment change. In the same way that feedback from a microphone into a PA system can turn an insignificant noise into an ear-piercing screech, changes within our environment may reinforce further environmental changes with potentially devastating effects.

Destroying our Planet to find Happiness is like chopping off our own limbs to lose weight

If you travel to the furthest realms of the earth's atmosphere you will eventually reach the point where the earth's gentle blues meets the blackness of the universe punctuated by the brightness of the stars. It is a beautiful and awesome sight, and for many, a life changing moment as the enormity and sheer brilliance of the Universe is an overwhelming reminder of our humanity. Are we really willing to risk it all and if so, for what?

CHAPTER THREE

THE GREEN DRESS

It was hanging in the middle of a popular department store. It wasn't particularly remarkable, special or expensive. It was simply a green dress. Yet, it changed my life.

In the days after my dad's death the initial mind-numbing shock was replaced with the reality of his funeral; what do you wear to the funeral of someone who has been such a fundamental part of your life? Fearing we had nothing suitable my mum sister and I decided to go shopping. Far from the usual joviality we wandered around the shops like bewildered sheep herded by our fellow shoppers. Eventually my sister encouraged me to buy a bright green dress. Although I was determined not to wear black, I was reticent. What would people think, and surely it would make my skinny ankles seem even skinnier and my bony arms, even bonier?

The dress was confined to its bag for three days before I finally showed my husband. After the usual interrogation I took a step back and reflected on my appearance in the mirror, my aching legs betraying how long I had stood there. Slowly my petty concerns faded into insignificance as I realised that life is simply too short not to wear 'our best' every day. My dad had spent the day he died shopping for holiday clothes which were to accompany him to Greece a few days later. The holiday never happened, when my parent's dreams were snatched from them. And it is the same for countless others at all ages.

When I talk about wearing 'our best', I am not really referring to clothes…although recognising myself for the fragile human being I am I know that dressing well helps me feel great. I am really talking about 'living' our best – for ourselves, our families and friends…the world. At that moment, wearing my green dress, I realised that I felt great, I looked great and I decided from that day forward I would wear 'my best' every day.

Months later I realised that the green dress moment had profoundly affected my well-being - my happiness, which was surprising because without doubt those same months had been amongst the most difficult and challenging of my life. This made me think very carefully about what it is that makes us happy. What was it about the 'green dress' moment that was so profound?

I knew it wasn't the green dress itself ... lovely though it was; it was just a dress. And I did not start spending money I couldn't afford on lots of clothes. However, I refused to accept second best. I refused to wear clothes which did not help me feel great, and in all areas of my life I tried to do my best.

A short time later I attended a local networking event to promote my business. The evening's speaker was an inspirational lady called Kath Temple. She had recently launched a magazine dedicated to the question of Happiness, entitled "Happiness, energy and spirit". I was soon struck by an article Kath had written about living your "Best Life". Kath talks about attending a prize giving evening at her daughter's school, coincidently the same school I had studied A Levels at. During the evening the head teacher said that "...he wants to be an outstanding husband, an outstanding father, an outstanding head teacher. And he wants that for his students too. That they strive to be outstanding, and give their very best in life."

I love the idea of doing our best with whatever situation we are in. It reminded me of my "green dress" moment. I wonder how many of us realise that despite our circumstances, wealth or status we can all chose to be outstanding. We can choose to be outstanding daughters, sons, parents, friends, brothers or sisters, colleagues and citizens. Or we can choose to be outstanding cleaners, solicitors, financial planners, secretaries, doctors or leaders. How different would life be if we chose this path "…that we each do our very best with what we have."

Instead we live in a World which despite half-hearted attempts to address other aspects of Wellbeing, still defines it by the money we earn and the economic success of the countries we live in.

Yet, we can hardly blame governments for measuring our happiness in this way. Frankly, the alternatives are frightening. Following the birth of my children, I had to complete the obligatory 'well-being' questionnaire with a health visitor. It was apparent that any negative response earned a black mark and a questioning gaze and soon I feared my medical records would be permanently blemished. The simple fact that I had cried since giving birth propelled me alarmingly quickly up the 'at risk' ladder. Of course, I had cried – having a child is one of life's most wonderful and most painful experiences. How, I wonder, would the Government go about the task of working out how happy its citizens are if measures of income and economic growth were abandoned? Few, I suspect, would willingly invite a member of the Government's Well-being Department into their homes.

Society measures success in an even more overt fashion. All you need is money regardless of whether you can afford to repay it. Then you can purchase the 'perfect' house, the trendy car, the most fashionable clothes, amazing holidays, the 'high life'...the list is endless and I am sure we all have our own ideas. Yet, we have seen little evidence that this is a very successful route to happiness. If you look at the rich list it is no secret that financial wealth often sits uncomfortably with happiness or well-being. Many people who have been successful financially have seen their personal lives marred by drug and alcohol addi- tions, marital and emotional breakdown and relational issues – hardly the making of happiness.

"...£10 million in the bank at 19. So what next?" de- clared a headline.

You could be forgiven for reading this article and think- ing that from now on this actress' life will always have less point – that now she is unlikely to have to worry about earn- ing a living her life will have less meaning. But the truth is at nineteen years of age her life is only just beginning. Years lie ahead of her; to explore the person she is; to de- velop her talents as an actress; to be an incredible friend; to be a great daughter...the possibilities are endless.

Unfortunately, we don't all have such concrete dreams. My debut as an actress was short lived when at the tender age of 5, I threw the baby Jesus across the stage in our pre- school nativity – a fact I am not allowed to forget. So how do we know what we really want? There's nothing quite like sitting at someone's funeral to make you think about the bigger questions in life. Its little wonder that most wakes feature easy access to alcohol; an opportunity to dull the senses and lighten the mood. As I listened to my dad's eulogy initially distracted by the honest and humorous account of his life, my thoughts wandered to what people may say about me if I died. What did I really want from life? Did I want people to see me as a good wife, mother and friend? Did I want people to see me as wealthy in the conventional sense? Did I want people to see me as stingy or generous? It's always saddened me that when I think of my paternal grandfather, I am reminded, not of the man who defended our country in the war, or taught my father to ride his bike, but the man who became so stingy in old age that we had to take our own tea bags with us when we visited. I think it was a surprise to my parents that when he died, he left enough money to buy a new house.

Reflecting on this I realised that the only rational response was to work out what I really wanted from life, and to align my day to day behaviour with these objectives and values. For instance, I realised that there is no point wanting to be a great mother if I do not spend enough time with my children. Equally, I realised that there is no point bemoaning some of the problems in the World if I am not prepared to do something about them.

More than that, I realised that the very definition of success means that we can define our success. We do not have to get caught by the insatiable trap of consumerism. We can determine our success by deciding what is important to us and working towards 'being successful' at it. If we seriously believe for example that the latest mobile phone model is going to make us happy or successful, we need to think again. The idea that any product or service will meet our deepest needs is doomed to fail. That does not mean that we should never have the latest mobile phone technology; the latest model may make it easier for us to achieve our goals; I simply couldn't run my life today without the technology which allows me to be a wife, mother and business leader. But I need to find a way to meet my goals without compromising my values.

I love this idea of success because it is very powerful; in the same way that we can choose to be outstanding we can literally write our own success stories. We don't need to be defined by the things we have acquired, or the titles we have. We don't have to have the 'best' house or the most fashionable clothes. We don't have to be terribly clever and have a top degree. We can be freed from the trappings of consumerism and decide what success means to us, and do our best to be successful at it.

Aside from "being my best" I think I now have a pretty good idea of what contributes to my well-being. Working with money has given me an insight into the lives of people who are wealthy in the conventional sense and I realise that a large bank balance, investment or property portfolio, or a well-paid job does not exempt people from life's ups and downs; financial "wealth" is not a one-way ticket to "happiness". In fact, frequently it causes worry; worry that banks may go bust; worry that the value of investments may tumble; worry about security of home and assets; worry about tax and so on. For me, I love leading a comfortable lifestyle – having loads is not important but not being able to afford a drink out with friends or the occasional treat makes me feel pretty miserable. I love my husband and children. I like to be my best. I like having time for family and friends. I like my house to look nice or (as family will testify) I get pretty grumpy, pretty quickly. It is important to me that I feel connected with people around me and to feel that people care about me. I love nature, I love sport, I love fresh air and I love spending time outdoors – walking, cycling and skiing are all good examples.

As I write this it strikes me that many of the things I love do not require endless amounts of money...or consumption. Yet many of the things that are important to me, and I expect many of us, are increasingly under threat because we are so obsessed with pursuing the traditional concept of happiness at any cost.

As we work ever harder, we compromise the limited time we have with our children before they grow up; as we make our organisations ever more efficient, we compromise our humanity; as we seek to protect ourselves from harm, we create a legalistic society and destroy trust; as pollution is emitted into the atmosphere, the quality of our air lessens; as we dump rubbish we spoil areas of natural beauty; as we endlessly develop tourist resorts we wave goodbye to little areas of paradise on Earth; as glaciers melt, opportunities to ski reduce; as we demand ever cheaper and cheaper goods, we condemn others to lives of misery...and so on it goes. Worse, we are facing the real danger that things we take for granted today in the developed world like food, water and shelter, may be compromised...in our ill minded pursuit of happiness.

Unlike me you may not be too unhappy that activities like skiing may not be around forever. You may also dismiss the cries of the world's leading scientists that we are heading for ecological disaster. But, are we really happy to accept that other people should face dire poverty and death because we cannot get to grips with what we really want from life?

Determined to stretch the boundaries of our monthly income beyond all known means, we are striving to consume more and more. We are not satisfied to eat, drink and pay the mortgage. We want to eat [a lot], drink [a lot], pay the bills and consume [a lot] more. We do not want to 'waste' money on life's essentials we want more.

An insatiable appetite is arguably one of the most common traits of the human disposition and one of our greatest

weaknesses. I have a weakness for crisps, particularly the
real potato, thick cut and seriously tasty variety which generally come in large family size bags. I tell myself that I
am only going to have a handful with a glass of wine one
evening. But once I've started, I don't stop, often eating
beyond the point of enjoyment. I've never looked at how
many calories there are in a packet of crisps and it's probably just as well. It certainly doesn't sit well with my
values to look after my health and waistline. Worse, is the
fact that my crisp bingeing sessions don't really satisfy me
– I am always disappointed by my greed. I admit that I felt
better recently as one of my colleagues recounted a story
of how he had consumed two whole tubs of a popular ice-
cream in one sitting; a whopping 2000 calories and 140
grams of fat later and he felt terrible. But it didn't stop him
eating through the whole Easter Egg we handed out to our
team at his desk.

Perhaps I should be grateful that I have a weakness for
food and not one for cars – it's certainly cheaper. But whatever we crave, it is perhaps one of life's greatest paradoxes
that its consumption cannot really satisfy our hunger. I
think that's because deep down we crave more than just
consumption of something in itself. Author, John Ortberg[4],
writes about a research group affiliated with the University
of Chicago who had recently listed the ten least happy jobs

[4] Taken from 'Soul Keeping' by John Ortberg Copyright ©
2014 by John Ortberg. Used by permission of Zondervan.
www.zondervan.com

in the world and the ten happiest. Their conclusion was simple; the ten least happy jobs were more financially lucrative and were associated with a higher status than the ten happiest jobs. They found that people in the happiest jobs had a higher sense of meaning – that they were coming home from work with a feeling of value and that this was more valuable than a big pay check. After all money can buy you many things to consume, but it can't buy the things that deep down we really crave.

So, we must ask ourselves whether there is a way we can be both happier in our own lives and less destructive in our lifestyles. I believe there is.

CHAPTER FOUR

BUSINESS AND MONEY;
not the root of all evil after all?

I have run my own business for over 10 years and I love it. Sadly, the fact that I work in the private sector is not always well received. It's no better when I explain that I work in financial services. In many people's eyes I have just gone from being materialistic and greedy to obsessed with money. In fact, when I started my career, training initially at an insurance company, and then for a firm of accountants dealing with the often more complex aspects of financial planning, I was criticised for choosing to work in the 'for profit' sector "surely, your talents are wasted there" or "why would you want to do that job?". It's true that this was also a time when, if the news was to be believed, financial advisers were less trusted than estate agents. In the late 90s the industry was still weighed down by the blight of endowment mis-selling. I had certainly not entered the profession at its height. But even then, a good financial adviser could make a massive difference to the wealth of his or her clients, and now, with levels of professionalism unrecognisable to the industry I entered, the right advice, makes a significant difference to the quality of people's lives both now and in the future. Yet, somehow, a work life dedicated to business is still seen as culturally less worthwhile.

Many of my friends work in the public sector and do not have this problem. Compared to the few minutes of polite silence following any brief discussion about my career, when they explain that they are a physiotherapist, or a nurse or teacher, it's met with enthusiasm; "how lovely…what age do you teach…where do you work. It must be very rewarding" and so on.

I recently attended the funeral of a close family friend who played a significant role in my childhood years. He had been the vicar of a parish in Nottingham and was a brilliant pianist and musician. Dedicating his life to the service of others he had died with few possessions but a massive estate of gratitude and love. He had four children. One of his sons, now a teacher working in a tough borough of London said that he thought his dad would be proud of the fact that he and his siblings had all decided to work in public services – to "better the lives of others" rather than the rather less worthy alternative. It had been an emotional day and I didn't challenge him but later I wondered whether I should have. Certainly, he was right that his dad would be proud of them, but not because of their choice of profession but because of who they had become.

Perhaps I should have asked why he felt that working in public services was more worthwhile but I suspect he's not alone. One of the things I love about my job is meeting and working with people from all walks of life to help them achieve their goals. Over the years I've met many people who have decided that they want to lead a more 'ethical' life. They too seem to share a common belief that by definition this means they should work in the not-for-profit sector; public services, charities, clubs and associations and so on.

This may be true for a minority but is conceptually flawed. Notwithstanding the fact that the World needs 'good' business people, those working in the not-for-profit sector, still need to consume goods and services to survive. Even households which are largely self-sufficient need lawyers to acquire land, or banks to lend money to them. Few people living outside our cities find it easy to get around without the use of a car and the services to keep them on the road. Even the most environmentally conscious struggle with issues surrounding transport as travelling has become an essential part of life for most of us. But importantly let's remember that without business the future looks very bleak as no business sector means no public sector. That means no hospitals, doctors or teachers – because who funds it? Yes, that's right, businesses who produce goods and services, (hopefully) pay corporation tax and pay their staff, who in turn pay all manner of taxes in the form of National Insurance contributions, income tax and VAT. We also need profits – a company which does not make any profits, is like a hen which does not lay any eggs. Pretty soon it will find itself redundant – in the case of the hen - served up for dinner. Profits are the lifeblood of business. They allow companies to grow, expand and innovate. And profits are taxed, allowing governments to provide essential public services; health and education, develop infrastructure and so on. Of course, what we don't need is companies who don't use their profits wisely, or use clever accounting techniques to avoid paying taxes.

I believe that good business is the future of us all. That good business is not a power for destruction but has the power to transform the World and better the lives of both the people working within it and the people it serves.

Similarly, many people don't understand the main principles of money, and rather than being its master, allow it to enslave them. I could write a book about people I've met who have been ruled by their wallets. In the nineties I worked with a lady who professed to hate the job she did, but when questioned why she didn't retrain or look for a new job, she said the company pension scheme was too attractive - she would never find the same benefits elsewhere. I was staggered, my senior by maybe twenty years, she was still a long way from retirement. I simply couldn't understand why she would do something she hated most of her waking life, just because of a pension scheme. Another friend maintained he couldn't afford to go out, and when he did, he would expect others to pick up the tab for him. I was annoyed when I realised he earned more than I did and still lived at home. He then puzzled why his social life stalled.

To be truly 'successful' in the modern World you need to learn to master money, rather than let it master you. You certainly can't function without it since it is the primary means of exchange (exchanging some for a couple of large glasses of wine in my local is one of my treats).

Whilst the concept of money as a means of exchange seems simple enough, explaining what it actually is, where it comes from and how it works – particularly in a global context, is far more complex.

A quick look at its history might help. Before money existed as we know it today people bartered to get the goods and services they wanted. For example, if I produced butter but had no bread and my neighbour had baked bread but had no butter, we could exchange some between us and both get what we need. But how would we barter today; things would get very complicated. Worse, how do you agree how many rolls of bread, a pound of butter is worth. Who knows? I would hate to work out how many rolls you need to purchase a car.

Problems like these led to the emergence of "Commodity Money". "Commodity Money" was an early form of money whose value derived from an actual commodity. Even today inmates in prisons exchange things like cigarettes in return for other 'goods'. But commodity money is inconvenient to store and transport. Imagine standing in your local supermarket isle with two trolleys – one laden with goods, another with cigarettes. It also does not allow governments to easily control or regulate business. Problems like these eventually spelt the end of exchanging actual commodities for goods and resulted in the emergence of "Representative Money". Representative money used coins and paper notes to represent real commodities stored elsewhere.

Gold was the most widely recognised commodity out of which to make money. It was compact, desirable and easily traded. It retains these characteristics today and is still regarded as a safe haven for investors in uncertain times. In 1844 the Bank Charter Act made the Gold Standard as the legal tender in Britain. This act gave the Bank of England the exclusive right to issue new bank notes, provided they were backed in full by Gold. There were 113.00159 grains (7.32g) of gold to one-pound sterling – roughly the weight of a fine gold chain or thin wedding ring. Unlike money as we know it today this gave it an intrinsic value – coins and notes were actually worth the amount of gold they represented.

The Gold Standard created trust – it helped people believe that money was more than 'fancy' paper; it had an exchangeable worth. In turn traders were willing to use bank notes as a means of exchange, knowing that they could always be redeemed for actual gold. So long as people continued to perceive gold as valuable all was well.

However, many countries were forced to abandon the Gold Standard including Britain in 1931. Amongst other problems it was difficult to mine enough gold meet the demands of growing economies. It was replaced by "fiat" money, which we still use today - although most of us probably associate "fiats" with small cars rather than money. "Fiat" money bears no relationship to any physical commodity and acquires its value in the same way as gold: simply from peoples' perception of value and faith that it can be used as a means of exchange. In some ways it is unnerving to think that we can place so much faith in money, when its value rests on such delicate foundations.

As "Fiat" money has no intrinsic value good management is vital. Consider, for example, what would happen in the UK if the Bank of England decided to increase the amount of money in circulation. Let's imagine that everyone gets £10,000 to spend. I can imagine frenzied scenes at my local shopping mall – people fighting over the entrance to the nation's favourite shops to spend their good fortune as internet servers are unable to keep up with the demand...only to find that prices have gone up significantly and their windfall isn't worth much.

To understand this, we need to remember that money is just a means of exchange – a way to 'share' a nation's goods and services – and since the activity of printing bank notes has not increased the nation's "store" of goods and services available for consumption prices must go up (or the value of money down) to maintain an equilibrium. 'Quantitative Easing' is a recent example of using the supply of money in a bid to control economies; governments terrified about deflation printed money to try and create inflation. Zimbabwe is a striking example of the effects that printing money can have as inflation hit two-hundred and thirty-one million percent in July 2008.

To conclude money is simply a means of consuming goods and services. And those with the most, get to consume the most.

But it strikes me that if half the world is hungry whilst the other half live in relative luxury, money is not exactly doing a great job as far as equality is concerned. So, what is going wrong?

It is not really money's fault that parts of the world are more 'developed' than others. This is the result of the complex evolution of history. The effects of the industrial revolution are perhaps most notable. It transformed the face of the UK and other economies by significantly increasing the output of goods and services, and, by doing so, eventually increasing general levels of wealth amongst these populations (albeit at a high cost to its labour force in early industrialised societies).

But if money is going to work for us today, we must consider its most fundamental flaw; the monetary cost of goods and services often does not reflect their true cost. This is a familiar concept in economics, yet we take little time to really consider what it means.

First imagine the contents of your grocery shop. When browsing the egg section, you face a choice – you can either buy half a dozen eggs for a pound or a different half a dozen for one pound, twenty-five. There is no discernible difference in their appearance. One is free-range, one is not. Which do you buy?

Imaging the next scene may be easier if you have read or watched 'The Birds' by famous novelist Daphne Du Maurier. There has been a revolution. Chicken-kind has secretly evolved and boasts an intelligence equal to humanity. It is going to make us pay for the cruelty and maltreatment of its species. No longer is it going to stand by while we cruelly neglect and imprison birds in battery cages.

The effects are devastating. People cannot leave their houses for fear of being pecked to death. Previously family destinations become a no-go zone. Farmers are driven off their land and in some areas food production halts. People suffer.

Unhinged by destruction and chaos, paying a small amount more for free range eggs is the bargain of the century.

What about coffee? Here, besides the sometimes-alarming choice of whether to buy caffeinated, de-caffeinated, mild, medium, strong or flavoured, we have to decide between fairly traded coffee and other brands. Which should we choose?

Now imagine that we can quantify the poverty and hardship faced by farmers earning a wage that even if they work every hour God sends their families will remain malnourished. Add this to the cost of exploitive coffee and giving coffee producers a fair share of the profits again seems a bargain.

It is not just the easy example of eggs and coffee; there are countless cases where the price of goods and services doesn't reflect their true price and suppliers are being exploited by the companies they supply but feel they don't have a choice.

An economist would argue that competition should keep prices at a level where there is just enough profit to make it worthwhile for the producers. But what if there are not any other types of work. Or what if other types of work mean that entire families have to join the millions who have already relocated to the slums of urbanisation, only to find that they face an equally terrible yet different fate.

We also need to understand that in low income Societies there is not much money to go around. It is easier for the rich to stay rich and for the poor to stay poor. This creates a devastating cycle of poverty trapping billions of people whilst an equally powerful cycle of wealth sees the minority of the World's population getting wealthier and wealthier.

Yet good business – and importantly, good economic growth – has the power to effect change.

In economics we talk about the 'multiplier effect' which is best explained by an example. Imagine you receive an unexpected bonus. You soon dream about how to spend your unexpected wealth and decide to buy a new car and spend the rest on a holiday. Your local car dealership uses the profits to pay its staff, who in turn go home to spend their wages. Meanwhile the hotel where you enjoyed your holiday can pay their staff on time (it has been a quiet season). To recap, your bonus is working hard. It has paid for a car and helped the dealership pay its employees. Your holiday meant the staff were paid on time allowing them to send money home to their families. And it does not end here - your money will continue circulating around the economy generating more 'wealth' as it goes.

Unfortunately, the converse is also true. This means that in poorer countries there is little wealth to go around. As easily as money can build wealth, it can sustain poverty.

No-one likes watching scenes of poverty on the television, and for most poverty is an uncomfortable subject we would prefer not to dwell on. It is easy to feel blameless for poverty and to a certain extent we are right; powerful forces, corrupt governments and policies mean that markets often do not function fairly. But it is important that we consider the role we can play.

It alarms me that we seem to be increasingly developing a taste for cheap(er) goods and services. Initially, it can seem very innocent – the theory goes that competitive markets should keep prices at a level which makes it worthwhile for both parties – the seller should make enough profit to make staying in business worth the effort, and the consumer should benefit from a great product or service at a good price. But we have a problem if we continuously demand cheap(er) goods.

There are different ways companies can deliver cheap(er) goods and one way is to cut costs. In recent decades many manufacturers have cut costs by relocating factories to countries with an abundant supply of cheap labour. This is hardly news, and there have been several cases where companies have been publicly 'tried' for the seemingly scant regard for the welfare of their workers.

A common response from a minority of people concerned about these issues is to avoid goods made in certain countries. This may ensure that we are not purchasing goods which have been produced under terrible conditions. However, we must understand that many countries want and desperately need this type of employment. A poorly paid, over worked person is still at least able to provide something for their family.

Another way to cut costs is to reduce quality. I have always fancied myself as an interior designer and took great delight in the purchase of my first sofa. Unlike my parent's traditional, boring, patterned sofa, my sofa was modern and trendy. However, my smugness was short-lived when less than three years later my sofa looked like it had spent its relatively short life as a bench on the London Underground. In contrast, even into their twenty-something year my parents' sofa still looked and felt like new. I 'suffered' my sofa for a further three years before the daily ritual of plumping up the cushions became too much to bear and I brought a new one. But sofas are just the tip of the iceberg. We recently had to replace our fridge freezer because we could not replace its seal which had split in several places. It had spent ten happy years in our kitchen, a fact I comforted myself with as I imagined the negative contribution I was making to the World's environmental problems, and I did feel vindicated when our friends said that they had been through several versions during the same ten years. But still I could not help my thoughts returning to the enormous amount of waste and wasteful behaviour prevalent in our Society and our sizeable contribution to the World's increasing wasteland in just a handful of years.

Worse, goods today are 'built to fail' to ensure a continuous cycle of purchasing – often at the detriment of our bank balances not to mention the environment. In addition to deliberately designing products to fail prematurely or become out-of-date, manufacturers may make it hard for consumers to repair their products, for example, by sticking components together or making it difficult to get access to replacement parts. Others add clauses to their user agreements so people (often unknowingly) agree not to fix their own products.

For consumers it means that the things we buy don't last as long as they should and even minor problems have to be dealt with by an approved repairer – often at greater expense, distance and delay, especially if we don't want to invalidate the warranty. For the environment it means we have ever-growing piles of waste as it is so much easier just to go out and buy something new than deal with the inconvenience and expense of having products fixed. The lifespan of electronic goods is certainly becoming shorter according consumer research with the number of defective appliances replaced within five years increasing in recent years.

The real problem lying behind these issues is that the environmental cost of producing goods and services is generally disregarded – we treat our natural World as it its dispensable and can be readily replaced. We ignore the unpleasant reality that we rely heavily on non-renewable resources and conveniently forget the potentially life changing cost of environmental destruction for future generations – often just for the sake of some cheap products. If environmental 'costs' could be factored into the price of the goods and services it would make no economic sense to unnecessarily replace products when they wear out or break down; it would always be cheaper to fix them.

According to an account written by well-known economist E F Schmacher, "every follower of the Budda ought to plant a tree every few years and look after it until it is safely established. The universal observation of this rule, [he remarks], would result in a high rate of economic development. The neglect of trees by contrast, causes the economic loss of whole countries[5]".

---

[5] 'Buddhist Economics', E F Schumacher, (1966)

By treating our environment as dispensable and failing to distinguish between renewable and non-renewable natural resources, we are exploiting nature to benefit the minority of the World's population. Worse, many of us don't even realise it.

The question is how can we transform the face of business so that we recognise its importance and value in a society and ensure that as far as possible it has a positive contribution to our world. And how can we handle our money so that it is working towards our goals, allowing us to be its masters and not its slaves?

CHAPTER FIVE

SUICIDAL SALMON

A small perfectly formed tear like a tiny freshwater pearl ran down my cheek and hung from my jaw. Soon they were like huge drops of rain silently splashing onto my desk. It was the final straw. I had worked tirelessly for months to hold everything together and now the tiredness I had ignored, which followed me like a shadow, over-whelmed me.

Isn't it funny how the little things tip the balance in the end? Holding it together through death and illness, suffer-ing and stress, it was my computer that 'broke' me in the end – or rather its inability to connect to the internet.

An impartial observer would have pointed out that none of the work I had to do couldn't wait a few more hours, and there were several solutions at hand. But with nerves worn to shreds no common sense remained. Crawling under my desk to check the hardware I found a tangled mess of wires and realised that I had no idea what to do. I should have made a calming cup of tea and telephoned for help but instead found myself laid prostrate on the floor giving into huge sobs which were now consuming my body.

For a while I contemplated ending it all. A feeling of relief engulfed me as I realised that never again would I have to deal with the incessant demands on my time and expertise, and the constant 'noise' that threatened to take over my mind, even in the middle of the night. Thankfully in those moments of despair there was nothing more dangerous to hand than an enormous tax reference guide and bludgeoning myself to death with this was unthinkable. Eventually the tears subsided and sense started to prevail. I thought of my family and feelings of despair turned to guilt. I sat up, reflecting on the fine line I had almost crossed, and prayed instead that God would kill me on the spot. Thankfully, this prayer remains unanswered.

On that awful morning I avoided becoming one of the fifty-eight hundred thousand recorded suicides each year in Europe; shockingly, more than the number of people killed on our roads. Perhaps this isn't surprising when depression is currently the main psychological disorder in the west and evidence suggests that it is increasing in almost every age group. If current trends continue, depression is expected to be the second most disabling condition in the world behind heart disease; hardly the making of happiness.

Stress is perhaps the most alarming trend in modern Society and one of the biggest causes because if one thing is certain, pursuing economic success in the lifestyles we lead and the houses we live in has put many of us under increasing strain as we work harder and harder to combine the pressures of family and working life; many of us forced into this lifestyle by the mortgages we secure on our homes.

"The clock is ticking. I have this unyielding sensation that time is passing by and I should be doing something. My life has become so complicated that the idea of doing nothing is untenable. I must do something. Perhaps I should return my telephone calls, catch up on my work, cook the dinner or tidy the house. Or maybe I should start working through my e-mails - tens of which are arriving by the hour, each sender expecting an instant reply. With no choice but to do everything as quickly as possible I feel like I am doing a good job of nothing. Where shall I start? I am so tired. I should not be surprised. With life's busy agenda who wouldn't be tired? If I could permit myself, I would crawl into bed and lie there hoping for this unending pressure to cease. But who am I kidding? Weighed down by this pressure I cannot sleep. Perhaps I should set an early alarm to maximise the productive hours of tomorrow..."

Author, John Ortberg, calls the struggle to fit everything in 'hurry sickness[6]'. I wonder how many of us are chronic sufferers? We try to cram so much into our days that even the things which should be enjoyable are not. We make decisions based on speed of execution, even if it isn't good for us. We drive when it would be better to walk, or we study the traffic always looking for the quickest lane; cursing if our decision turns out to be poor or if the driver in front has the audacity to drive slowly in the fast lane – the traffic in the slow lane mocking us with its rapid progress. Perhaps we don't make time for lunch so we grab a meal on the run trying to ignore the nagging feeling that yet more fast food is doing nothing for our waistlines. Or we make that last phone call when really we should be leaving for an appointment, and find ourselves making pathetic excuses for our tardiness when we know we just didn't leave enough time.

In the early days of my career I felt like I earned a degree in hurriedness and busy-ness often thanks to the challenge of combining work and family life. There's the time a client rang just after I had collected my daughter from nursery. My daughter needed the toilet and it was clear that there was no time to waste. Deep down I knew I should ignore the call but sadly my pressured brain

[6] Taken from 'Soul Keeping' by John Ortberg Copyright © 2014 by John Ortberg. Used by permission of Zondervan. www.zondervan.com

convinced me otherwise; scenes of dismissal and professional tribunals sprang to mind, my reputation in tatters...Of course it was nonsense, but, stressed, I was unable to make a good decision. That's why I found myself on my phone at the side of the road, and my daughter, whom I had bribed with a sweet to stay quiet, dangling between my legs doing a wee. On other occasions I turn into the mother from hell as I scream at my children for a minor offense simply because I am stressed.

I expect we can all recall a time when stress has affected our behaviour. Perhaps a work project gradually takes over our thoughts and minds; and before long its importance becomes blown out of all proportion. We become so single minded in its pursuit that we compromise all that is really important to us to get the job done, even our health. Or perhaps we miss important events and special occasions because of a task we have trouble recalling just a few months later. Too easily our emotional & physical wellbeing is put on a back seat to profit-making or 'achievement'. We come to believe that it is more important to hit 'targets' than to care for others and ourselves. It doesn't help when we are told that illness and injury cost our economies staggering amounts each year. Sadly, we don't realise what a mockery these figures are. Our bodies were never designed to work endless hours under increasing amounts of stress. They are like cars. They need regular servicing or they break down – or they may be serviced with the upmost of precision but they break down anyway.

At least we can fix our cars reasonably easily. Shame we can't say the same of our bodies or broken relationships. Expecting one hundred per cent efficiency is like planning a budget without a contingency; it is crazy. Yet, we have a culture which rewards attendance at any cost even in our schools, where certificates are awarded for good attendance and even genuine illness can mean that kids miss out on rewards. Of course, we want people to work hard and not skive off, but we need a culture which avoids spreading nasty germs, and allows people to feel they can take time off when they are ill. It's crazy to work so hard for money that it damages our health, with the irony that often it has to be fixed at great cost.

How many of us can look at cultures of the organisations we work for and feel proud of what they represent. There is often much to be desired; overtime is the norm; leaving the workplace on time is frowned upon; taking time off is discouraged; mums and dads miss their children's Christmas plays; people do not take all their holiday entitlement for fear of appearing lazy; and even genuine absenteeism can buy you a one-way ticket to demotion. I recently met a lady who was considering early retirement because her working environment had become intolerable – amidst staff cuts and increasing workloads she saw her target increase twofold. The resultant stress was literally breaking down her health one nerve at a time.

Worse impossible targets and endless to do lists are not limited to the private sector; doctors, nurses, teachers, social workers, police officers, to name a few, seem to be working under increasing pressure. It seems to have become part of our culture that enormous workloads are the norm; staffing levels are kept to the minimum and everyone is terrified of being sued.

Under this kind of pressure, it is not surprising that more and more people are struggling with issues of stress and depression - yet good mental health should be a starting place for well-being. You could be sitting in a hot tub at the world's most luxurious resort, sipping an ice-cold glass of Champaign, but if you are stressed or depressed it will cloud everything that would otherwise be so enjoyable; the sun may appear dull, the drink tasteless and laughter may feel like a distant memory. It's like having a fog descent on your life which clouds everything until it becomes impossible to see through it.

Rather than caring about our emotional wellbeing our culture defines it by the clothes we wear, the cars we drive and the houses we live in. As long as we can tick these boxes we are 'doing well for ourselves' – we are 'successful'. In a world where it's more important to look good on the outside than feel good on the inside perhaps it is inevitable that more and more people – people from all walks of life - are struggling with drug and alcohol addiction. I often look with sadness at my teen heroes – singers, actors, actresses whom I longed to be like; people who in the traditional sense have been more 'successful' than they could have ever imagined; people, who after years of drug abuse, remain shadows of who they once were

It is true that many of life's joys come in the simplest of ways. When my children were young, I loved watching them play in the garden. If truth be told it was a bit of stretch to call it a garden. Landscaped by the previous owner, it would have been more accurate to describe it as an urban space, complete with the inevitable water feature, several large stones and thousands of pebbles. The only greenery was a beautiful wisteria bush which required endless pruning to tame it – and the blackened remains of once glorious mimosa trees sadly killed by subzero temperatures a previous winter. Nonetheless this small space was of significant amusement to our children and allowed them to run around, shrieking with laughter away from the sometimes-claustrophobic interior of our home. Their delight in the 'garden' often lasted significantly longer than the allure of their numerous toys. I guess I shouldn't be surprised – I spent my childhood running around our larger garden and then in later childhood when my parents moved to a larger house and inevitable smaller garden – the modern compromise – my brothers and I spent our spare time in the local woods where we would make dens and climb trees.

Sadly, we, along with many other parents were scared to let our children outside the confines of our gardens and into our local communities. Frankly, living on the outskirts of a city, until my children started school, I had trouble remembering my neighbours' names, let alone who lived a couple of doors away. Who knew who might be lurking around the corner waiting to harm them? So instead of participating in our local community we fill our houses with expensive technology that allows us to simulate the outdoors in our living rooms. Naturally, flicking ones' wrists up and down as fast as possible is the same as learning to kick a ball, play tennis or run a marathon. Or maybe rather than enjoying a cup of coffee and a chat with our neighbours we have virtual friends and measure our popularity and success by how many connections we have on popular social networking sites. It is not a problem if we don't actually see them. As long as we share a few messages from time to time all is well. Far easier in fact that the often-messy reality of human relationships. We don't think about what it means to be human forgetting that we are designed to live in community with each other. Perhaps that's why many of us live in our little 'boxes' and too easily lead isolated and lonely lives.

"Being unwanted, unloved, uncared for, forgotten by everybody, I think that is a much greater hunger, a much greater poverty than the person who has nothing to eat."

Mother Teresa

I wonder how many people sit in their comfortably furnished homes with everything they could ever need and
more materially yet are emotionally impoverished; men
and women who spend every waking moment at work because of the loneliness that awaits them at home, the
welcome mat a cruel reminder; mums stuck in for hour after hour with young children with little company apart from
the characters of their children's favourite TV programme;
the elderly hidden behind closed doors.

We then puzzle at scenes of joy from countries where
materially people have so little or communities where people have chosen to live without modern comforts. Can it
be true that despite financial constraints many communities
living in 'poor' countries are richer than we could ever imagine; richer in trust; richer in joy; richer in community
spirit; richer in friendship?

Perhaps the biggest threat to our society (and time) is
our increasingly legalistic culture. It is the fear of being
sued, an increasingly trust-less and bureaucratic society
that has seen almost every industry swamped in paperwork.
Many of us work with the real possibility that we spend
longer filling out paperwork or writing reports to cover our
backs than we do looking after the needs of our clients, customers and patients. I certainly do. The financial services
industry is awash with bureaucratic nonsense in the name

of consumer protection. The irony is that often endless box ticking does little to make sure people are getting a good deal. In the UK, fixated on the realms of red tape for day to day business, during the 2008 financial crisis our regulatory authorities overlooked the issues within our financial sector which brought the high street banks to their knees. I am sure that my clients were reassured by my meticulous reports and detailed paperwork, and didn't mind at all that they almost lost every penny of their savings in the bank.

Life is certainly harder without trust. One year I was interviewed by the UK financial regulator to assess how well my firm had implemented their latest initiative. We sailed through the questions with surprising ease until what seemed a trick question; "How do we know you look at your management information?" As I pondered the question, I wondered whether CCTV was to become a regulatory requirement and my colleagues and I would be watched over in our office by Big Brother – no more sneaky coffee breaks and chocolate biscuits. Or perhaps it was a wind-up and any moment someone was going to jump out of the filing cabinet with a television camera and tell me it was a joke; sadly not. To reassure them that I read the reports I prepare each month, they recommended that I should 'talk' to myself about them and minute the outcome. As I took their comments on board trying to keep the despair I felt from my expression I couldn't help but feel as though I could spend every hour or my professional life covering my back but never get around to actually doing my job – of looking after and advising people about their money. Somewhere a line has to be drawn.

At least its only money; in our hospitals I am sure doctors and nurses spend hours completing paperwork to cover their backs to the detriment of patient care and attention. Twice, I have been rushed into theatre for surgery. The first time was during the final and complicated throws of labour. Before proceedings could begin, I had to sign the obligatory consent form. What a waste of time; I was barely conscious - I would have signed anything. The second time I needed emergency surgery. The paperwork had been carefully prepared with all the risks explained in some detail, the following consultation with the surgeon akin to some bizarre sales process. At the end I asked a simple question – what happens if you don't operate? The consultant seemed to struggle for words – who can blame him - no one likes to talk about death. Not much of a choice. Twenty-four hours later and I would be dead. If patient consent is needed in situations like these couldn't we have a 'please save my life' form, and I accept the consequences.

But sadly, more and more we bring this bureaucracy which fills our working days, fuels our stress levels and wastes our time, on ourselves. It is the increasingly legalistic and selfish nature of our society which tempts us to make a quick buck when we trip over a crack in the pavement and, unfortunately, genuine claims are often marred with the same brush. A friend of mine was harassed into a personal injury claim because despite her assurances that she had not suffered any injury during a minor car accident the 'ambulance chasers' would not leave her alone. After being pestered all week she gave in, uttering a tired and resigned acknowledgement that perhaps she had felt some discomfort. Afterall, who would ever know?

It is not just the culture of our organisations which can fall short, many people struggle with the quality of their working lives. Many of us will recall our childhood ambitions. At the age of five I decided that I wanted to be a nurse. Given that I tend to faint at the slightest sight of blood it's a good thing that I changed my mind and wanted to be a teacher; later ambitions included journalism, architecture and banking. I never dreamt of being a call centre operative or a data processor and I doubt many people do. Yet many people do mind numbingly boring jobs. Of the 3 billion workers in the World I wonder how many are bored out of their minds, all day long?

There is no doubt that we owe the material wealth of the modern world to Adam Smith's 'division of labour'. Using the example of a pin factory in pre-industrial Britain Smith described how dividing a job up into several separate and distinct tasks can significantly increase output. Bearing in mind that at the time of writing most goods were made by small groups of three or four people, he wrote:

> *"...the trade of the pin-maker...could scarce, perhaps, with his upmost industry make one pin in a day, can certainly could not make twenty. But in the way which this business is now carried on, not only the whole work is a peculiar trade, but it is divided into a number of branches...One man draws out the wire, another straights it, a third cuts it, a fourth points it, a fifth grinds at the top for receiving the head; to make the head requires two or three distinct operations; to put it on, is a peculiar business, to whiten the pins is another; it is even a trade by itself to put them into the paper; and the important business of making a pin is, in this manner, divided into about eighteen distinct operations, which, in some manufactories, are all performed by distant hands...I have seen a small manufactory of this kind where ten men only were employed, and where...each person...[averaged] four thousand eight hundred pins a day. But if they had all wrought separately and independently, and without any of them having been educated to this peculiar business, they certainly could not each of them make twenty, perhaps not one pin in a day[7]".*

Smith is describing how a day's output in a simple pin factory can increase exponentially simply by dividing up the work into many different tasks, each capable of being repeated many times over in one day. By using this process of specialisation workers tend to get better and better at performing their dedicated task, even, Smith argued, to the extent where they may develop their own inventions to help

---

[7] 'The Wealth of Nations', Adam Smith, 1776

them. If this sounds familiar it should. Over the last century many countries have been through a process of industrialisation (and technological advance) which has seen overall levels of output increase exponentially, and with it, general levels of wealth. But even Adam Smith acknowledged the dangers of the excessive "division of labour". He feared that too much specialisation may rob workers of their intelligence and wit:

> "The man whose whole life is spent in performing a few simple operations, of which the effects too are perhaps, always the same...has no occasion to exert his understanding, or to exercise his invention...He, naturally, therefore loses the habit of such exertion, and generally becomes as stupid and ignorant as it is possible for a human creature to become.[8]"

In today's economies I fear that we have forgotten Smiths' warning. Our focus on producing ever increasing quantities of goods and services to prop up economic growth has created thousands and thousands of dull, repetitive jobs. Mass production techniques have divided work into many small, dull and menial tasks, reducing skilled craftsmen to mere parts of a machine. People have been moved from offices to call centres, doomed to answer hundreds of calls a day within strict timescales. I was once asked by a call centre operative to ring back separately about each of my clients' eight pension and life assurance

---

[8] 'The Wealth of Nations', Adam Smith, 1776

policies because she had just two minutes allowance for each call. The ten-minute wait to be connected and frosty reception preceding this news did not make my day. In other industries workers have timed toilet breaks – it is little wonder that we need drugs to control our bodily functions. It is perhaps also not surprising to learn that depression is a significant cause of absenteeism.

We need to ask ourselves whether we are compromising our humanity in an ill-conceived pursuit of happiness. In our efforts to chase economic growth and produce as much as possible as efficiently as possible with as little risk as possible have we forgotten what we are working for? Despite daily targets, organizational hype and never ending to do lists, work is a means to provide us with water, food, clothing and shelter. But what's more, done well, work is a means to provide us with satisfaction and purpose, an opportunity to come together with other people in a common task and contribute to the World around us. To treat it as something to eliminate, to rid ourselves of; a burden, is to fail to recognise the important contribution it can make to our own happiness. And to treat it in a way which makes jobs boring and meaningless is to forget our humanity.

You may be wondering what Salmon has to do with all this. It's at the height of a Salmon's prime that with clockwork precision, nature calls her home to lay her eggs. Years of life in the ocean help prepare her for the long journey. To reach the freshwater streams of her birth, she amazes us with her abilities; swimming thousands of miles against rapid currents with satellite precision and leaping up waterfalls like a highly trained athlete.

Finally, she arrives. The tremendous feat is worthwhile. Huge relief is shared with other mothers-to-be as the eggs are laid. Yet within hours of giving birth the Salmon will die. From the most amazing achievement of her life to death in such a short time; it's a sobering thought.

It seems a terrible injustice that the most amazing feat of a Salmon's life leads her to her death. Perhaps as she tires from the long journey, she realises the impact on their health. Maybe she can feel her body slowly shut down as she focuses all her efforts on the goal, realising too late that death is inevitable.

Few of us, I am sure, would be motivated to pursue a dream which spells certain death. Yet, without change, the objects of our desires may be the same thing to destroy us all. Even if we survive the damaging effects of mass consumerism on our health and natural environment, can we live with the effects on society? And so, we must ask ourselves whether we are doomed to chase after the alluring scent of consumerism until it has literally brought us to our knees, or do we have the stomach for change? And if we are willing to change, what type of change do we need?

Doubtless, we need clever people to develop more sustainable models for our economies, but what if the real power to change the world lies within us each?

Adam Smith, once commented on the power of man's selfish pursuits. Few would be so naïve to think that the shop owner is only motivated by the joy of his work. He works hard to satisfy other people's desires so that he can enjoy the profits of his labour; "...he intends only his own gain; and he is in this, as in many other cases, led by an invisible hand to promote an end which was no part of his intention[9]."

What if we could use our own self-interest in ways which are constructive, instead of destructive? What if the answer to the environmental and social problems we face is not to leave it to someone else but to better understand what makes us successful, to turn our back on society's definition of success and boldly work to become truly successful in our own lives?

---

[9] 'The Wealth of Nations', Adam Smith, 1776

CHAPTER SIX

I JUST WANT TO BE HAPPY

For a long time, I suffered from a regular bout of the blues; something I coined 'The Sunday Night Feeling'. At best, it was described as the feeling that comes with the end of the weekend; at worst, it was a feeling of dread that soon it would be Monday morning and for me the usual 5 day working week would commence. On good days I would shrug it off as easily as an unnecessary layer of clothing on a hot day. On bad days it would consume me and despite my best efforts I was unable to escape its suffocating effects.

I no longer suffer from the Sunday Night Feeling – in fact, I've not suffered for years. I still do the same job. A job I've always loved. The difference is that rather than continue to ignore my dream of running my own business – something that would have been easy to do, I pursued it.

The timing was horrible. The Credit Crunch induced recession was just starting to bite and the financial world was in crisis; hardly the right time to launch a financial planning firm with no clients to speak of and a family to provide for – the youngest of which was just eight months old. The night before my resignation I had serious misgivings and told my husband that I should stick with my job – after all, I was not only a working mother – I was the main breadwinner. He has a habit of cutting straight to the point and simply said "What's the worst that can happen?". Images of us begging for food sprang to mind and feeling cross I accused him of being glib. But even I had to admit that I was overreacting. I was not only a financial expert, adept at finding my way out of most financial challenges, I had never been out of work and had frequent offers of employment. The worst-case scenario, if I was honest, was that I would either have to beg for my job back or find another. Hardly the end of the world. I agreed that it would be a shame to waste all the months I had spent planning and went for it.

Hindsight is a wonderful thing and it would be easy now to forget the heartache and sheer hard work that's seen the business grow over the years – several of which I earned very little as I juggled work and childcare, determined to ensure that my dreams of being a business woman didn't compromise my family values. Yet I realised later that the start of my business coincided with the death of the Sunday Night Feeling. Over a decade later I still feel motivated and energised by the challenges facing me every day. More than that is a deep sense of satisfaction which sustains and enriches my life.

Realising goals, ambitions and dreams may not always be possible or even desirable. My, at the time, ten-year-old daughter proudly announced that she was going to audition for a famous talent show. I was in her bad books when I had to ask what talent she planned to showcase. Believe me, the World would not have been enriched by her debut as a singer and I refused to be the parent egging her on the side-line when a singing career for her was a likely as snow in Britain in August (although maybe climate change will change this in the future). Later, though, she developed a love of gymnastics but was reluctant to join a club. When I asked why she said that she was never going to be an Olympic gymnast so what was the point? I agreed that starting in her teens meant that getting to the Olympics was unlikely but asked whether she was missing the point. If you love it you should do it, I advised. Not long later as I picked her up from her first session she bounced into the car, joy simply radiating from her. Eighteen months later she won a Gold medal at her first competition but more importantly, training in the gym is something she loves and helps balance the pressures of school and study as she prepares for her GCSEs.

In adulthood, however, it's easy to forget the things that once brought us joy and instead fill our lives with distractions. As a child I played the piano, and just as my daughter loves gymnastics, I loved it. I doubt now that it blessed my family, particularly as I learnt my scales, practicing over and over again until I could play them perfectly – but it brought joy and satisfaction to my life. Despite this I stopped playing in my twenties and, distracted by my studies and quest for both academic achievement and career progression, it was years before I took it up again. Strangely it wasn't until I did that I realised how much I missed it. I felt almost that I had lost part of myself for all those years.

Another childhood joy was helping my dad in the garden. I remember painting the garden shed with him in the first family home I have any concrete memories of in Hove, England. I'm not sure how much help I really was, and suspect now with the understanding that comes with age and experience that he tolerated my help and was secretly pleased when I got bored and reverted to riding my bicycle round and round the small square of paving, which stood centre stage encasing a small flower bed, until I got dizzy. My youngest daughter who also loves gardening, really blessed me at the age of three when she pruned all the flower heads from my rose bushes. "Mummy" she exclaimed as I was busily pruning a large shrub "look how I've helped!" After rushing to remove the oversized scissors from her tiny hands which she had snuck into the garage to borrow I wasn't sure whether to laugh or cry.

I rediscovered my love of gardening in my thirties. Without doubt one of the things I love most is a garden's ability to give pleasure often years after the original investment of time and money. When we moved into my current property the garden was in a state. It was clear that some years before the house had been owned by a talented and enthusiastic gardener and as we cut back the ivy and fought with years of unchallenged bindweed, we discovered many hidden 'treasures' including a dragon sculpture. We were not so blessed by the rickety wooden bridge rising above an oversized pond. Two days after we moved in, I gave birth to my third and youngest child and shortly after it snowed heavily. One morning I came downstairs to find my older two daughters had crept into the garden and were jumping up and down midway on the bridge as it precariously creaked under their weight. Needless to say, the pond and bridge are now gone and visitors will find a rock garden in its place.

Whilst I certainly enjoyed designing and replanting my garden, the satisfaction and joy I get from it has only increased over time. It's like a product which keeps on giving, well after the initial purchase. There is no comparison to the short-lived satisfaction and joy which comes with most purchases. Yet often I am tempted to buy things which give me a quick fix when really, I know that I should focus on the things which bring long term satisfaction and joy. It's the same with relationships. How easy it is to reach for a quick consumer fix when we feel down rather than invest in the relationships which can doubtless bring us far more joy and satisfaction in the long term.

Perhaps that's why it's so easy as we grow up to forget the things which bring us joy. I asked myself why I stopped playing the piano. The answer was simple; I had been lying to myself. I told myself I didn't have time; my schedule was too busy with work, study and family commitments. How could I possibly find time to do the things I enjoyed? And, who was setting me such tough deadlines that I didn't have time for anything else? That's right, it was me. I set my schedule and in a crazy sadistic way I cut out key things I really loved.

I think initially I thought I would find more joy in the things that I would achieve through my studies and career progression. It's certainly true that with a steady career path the amount I earned gradually grew allowing me to purchase some of the things that I thought would be better. The sad fact is that they weren't. We have nurtured this culture which teaches us that joy and happiness is related to what we have. At every stage of our lives we are conditioned to consume; our children are tempted with 'kiddies meals', trendy toys, games and even clothes; in early adulthood we join the race for happiness by driving the right car, having the latest furniture, wearing the right clothes and living in the right house; in later adulthood bored with buying things for ourselves we may indulge our children and grandchildren. But too often we work within these predefined ideas of success often with little idea of what success means to us and too often we forget the simple things which bring us joy.

I love travel and can spend hours researching possible holiday destinations with the aid of a list of things which I've learnt are important to us. Within walking distance of a bar or restaurant is a must, as is easy access to swimming, sports and leisure activities. Other requirements, such as a beautiful garden, are nice to have but not essential. Then there's the list of things we can happily go without – for me, that includes WIFI (but not all the family agree).

I find it fascinating that it's so easy to spend time like this planning our holidays and taking care to choose some-where which ticks the right boxes, but don't take time to plan our own lives. I guess it's easier to distract ourselves than face the somewhat more challenging question of what to do with our lives and, face up to the changes we may need to consider.

Equally, when someone's life is taken away or a loved one is seriously ill, it is easy to appreciate how mundane many of the things we occupy ourselves with really are. Daily tasks slide into insignificance when we face the ques-tion of life and death. With this comes an urgency to pursue those things that are really important; relationships; community; our gifts and talents; the extraordinary beauty of our World and the sheer joy of being alive...

But reminders like this are unwelcome and at the hectic pace of our modern lives, it is all too easy to spend time on things or to consume things which bring instant gratification rather than long term satisfaction. It is widely recognised, for instance, that when we are stressed, we tend to make poor food choices; we drink too much tea and coffee; we crave sweets, chocolate and crisps; we fill up on 'junk' food. I should know, looking after client's investments can be stressful, particularly at times of international crisis; the financial crisis was challenging enough, the Covid-19 crisis has been remarkable for all the wrong reasons. In these particularly turbulent Stock market conditions I can easily revert to scoffing all the chocolate I can find in my cupboards (even the cooking chocolate), knocking back large glasses of wine and eating junk food. The irony is that bad food choices create more stress for my body and actually make me feel worse, contributing little for my health and fitness – something that is really important to me.

With stress we also tend to make bad choices about how we spend our time. Really important things, like our families, friends and spouses take a back seat to sending 'a quick e-mail' or just finishing 'that last little job'. The trouble is that before we even realise it, an hour has passed and we have lost the chance to read our children their bedtime story, or ask a partner about their day. The old mantra that no one on their death bed ever says that they wish they had spent more time at work is doubtless true, but how do we work out what we really want from our lives – what will make us truly happy?

Maybe, like me, something is stopping you from pursuing something you love. What lie are you are telling yourself? What is your 'Sunday Night Feeling'? What does success look like for you? Maybe you are tempted to work to the World's idea of success but don't feel very successful inside.

I was invited to an 'invite only' dinner recently for senior managers and business owners of financial planning firms, held at a five-star hotel just outside London. My dilemma was simple. Unable to travel by train on this occasion it made sense to drive our hybrid, very efficient car to the event rather than our newer, larger seven-seater diesel powered and much less environmentally friendly car used to transport our children and their friends around. The thing was that I had argued with a lamppost the week before with the result that my little hybrid now sported a nasty dent across its side and rust was already making its home where the paint had been removed and it was awaiting repair. I was worried that my reputation as a successful business owner may be tarnished by my damaged and frankly non-executive car. But I also felt that I should stick to my values – one of which is to limit my impact on the environment as much as possible. I was really torn. But eventually I decided on the hybrid.

Acres of lush gardens greeted me as I made my way along the drive to where the hotel rose impressively from the grounds, the car seeming to glide silently in electric mode allowing me to enjoy the call of the countryside around me until I caught up with the car in front whose engine drowned out any trace of nature. Admittedly, I chose not to use the valet service – I think my car would have looked out of place amongst the many gleaning, impressive models ahead of me – but I was proud of myself for not bowing to the perceived pressure I felt. I may not have looked very successful on the outside, but I certainly felt it on the inside and without doubt that's what's really important.

For me, I think that's where true happiness really lies. It isn't in the things I own or consume, it's in the way that I feel inside, it's in a deep part of me which no one else can see or judge. Maybe that's why happiness often comes in the least expected ways and the causes of such happiness can be equally difficult to predict. For instance, there is lots of evidence that giving things away – whether its money, possessions or your time, can be a great source of happiness. My accountant thinks I'm nuts but one of the things I really enjoy is sharing some of the profits from our business. I have never regretted giving money away and think that the World would be a much better place if more businesses and people did.

In the early years of my business I belonged to a global business network. Aside from the fact that members of my family coined it the 'sadist club' because I had to get up at 5am to be there shortly after 6, its built on a fantastic motto of 'givers gain'; a concept which has seen it grow from humble origins to an international business success with over a quarter of a million members across the World at the time of writing. The principle is that by focusing on finding and referring business for other trusted professional members, your own business will succeed as you grow and develop your contacts until there is a whole network of people recommending your services. By giving of themselves and their time, its members really do have an opportunity to gain. However, it takes time. Relationships do not happen overnight and anyone who wanted to join, make a lot of contacts and money but was not willing to invest in the people around them was doomed to fail.

Perhaps that's why happiness can be so elusive. Maybe, contrary to modern culture, it's in the giving of ourselves that we can truly gain, just not in the way we imagined. I expect we can all recall times when we feel unexpectedly happy in the most mundane of circumstances – it happened to me the other day. It was a perfectly ordinary day. Nothing exciting or remarkable was happening, I was simply walking down my street holding my daughter's hand as I was struck with an extraordinary sense of wellbeing as I was reminded what a precious gift it is to be a parent. This simple joy was like a bubble of euphoria which lifted my

spirits, put a spring in my steps and left me humming qui-
etly to myself for the rest of the day (much to the annoyance
of my colleagues).

There are many accounts where people have discovered
happiness in the most difficult of circumstances. Victoria
Milligan's life changed forever when she and her family
were involved in a speed boat accident in Padstow, Corn-
wall killing her husband and daughter and leaving her with
life changing injuries and responsibility for her three sur-
viving children. Yet even though she would give anything
to hug her husband one more time or read her daughter another bedtime story, she says that it has helped her learn to
appreciate life in a new way and live in the moment as she
never could before. She describes of how she now literally
stops to smell the roses in her garden, whereas before she
never had time and was always rushing around to host
whatever birthday party or friends were over, never really
appreciating the beauty of the environment around her[10].
So where should we really be looking for happiness? What
beauty are we rushing by, failing to appreciate the joy that
it can bring to our lives. What gifts, talents or recreations
are we ignoring, and plastering over with cheap imitations
of happiness and short-term highs?

First and foremost, we need a new definition of our own
success and, on a global scale, of economic success. We

---

[10] http://victoriamilligan.co.uk/, Victoria Milligan (2015)

need to demand policies which create and support what we truly value in life instead of the things Society tells us we should value. We need to embrace the idea of caring; caring for our natural environment; caring for each other as families, friends, communities and employees; caring for our living environment; and caring for our future. Nothing has illustrated the benefits of caring quite so well as the differing response to the Covid-19 crisis with some communities coming together to support others, clap for carers, and look after each other, and others, with neighbours turning on each other and reporting people to the police for violating rules before even attempting to understand what is going on in each other's' lives.

We must abandon the foolish idea that we will only be happy if we can consume endless amounts of material possessions – so many things in fact that our houses are fit to burst and get back to what is really important in our lives. We need to take the time to understand what this means to us each individually. It will be no mean feat. We need radical change. Nothing else will be enough. The environmental issues we face demand a rethink of Local, National, and International policy. We need Governments that are willing to embrace the real issues of the day, without getting side-tracked by popularity contests. And we need to support these Governments.

Crucially, we need systems that do not rely on an endless amount of material consumption to be "successful".

We still need economic growth but we need a different type than we have been conditioned to believe is good for us. We need life giving economic growth. We need economic growth which does contribute to our well-being. We need economic growth which does not create thousands of poor quality goods at the expense of our beautiful planet. We need economic growth which meets our needs without leaving over half of humanity hungry and thirsty.

Importantly the type of change we need does not start and stop with Governmental policy. It is easy to play the blame game. Of course, it is not our fault, how can we do anything differently when no-one cares about our views? It is our governments – they are corrupt. It is our businesses – they are taking advantage of us. It is our public services – they are wasting our money. It's so easy to play the blame game but, despite the elements of truth that inevitably lie behind statements like these, we must accept that we are all responsible – as families, communities, employees, Civil Servants, Businesses, Politicians, Nations and ultimately, as individuals.

Crucially, we need to develop corporate structures where the businesses that provide us with the goods and services we need are not just money-making machines, with little or no regard for anything else. We need to create a culture where businesses are entities that creatively provide and distribute goods and services; businesses that creatively employ; businesses that give; businesses that excel without costing the planet.

Because good business, I believe, has the power to change the World. And to support good business we need creative consumers and what I like to call creative consumerism.

Creative consumerism is about aligning our consumption habits with our personal values. It is about recognising what we really need in life, rather than what we think we want. It is about living a life that is really dedicated to the pursuit of things that can deliver true happiness and contentment, rather than playing the ever-exhausting game of consumerism – where more will never be enough. Creative consumerism is about sending the right message to companies. It is about putting people, and our amazing planet before money.

Whilst destructive consumerism cares only about getting as much as possible as cheaply as possible, creative consumerism values the people and the natural resources involved in the process. Destructive consumerism ignores quality, and cares only for short term profits. Creative consumerism demands and creates quality, and is interested in long term rewards. Destructive consumerism creates waste. Creative consumerism reduces waste. Destructive consumerism treats nature and living creatures as expendable, creative consumerism seeks to work in harmony with nature and living creatures. Destructive consumerism competes only on price.   Creative consumerism competes on value – valuing nature and life and providing a competitive product or service without compromising our core values.

We must abandon the excuse that our actions will merely be the actions of a few and cannot really make a difference. I once heard the story of a little boy walking along the beach. Washed up onto the beach were tens of thousands of Starfish, who, without escape to the cooling waters of the Sea would soon be dead in the scorching heat of the day. Upon learning this, the little boy started throwing the Starfish one by one back into the Sea. An observer ridiculed him for his actions, pointing out that he could not possibly make a difference to the fate of the Starfish. The little boy responded simply by bending down, picking up a Starfish and throwing it back into the water. "Made a difference to that one" he said. He picked up and threw another into the Sea, "and that one".

Rory Spowers, writer and broadcaster, writes in his book 'A Year in Green Tea and Tuks-Tuks':

> *"We have been conditioned to believe that the individual has been completely disempowered and there is little he or she can do to prevent the inevitable… That is precisely the notion we need to confront, as we work towards a new definition of 'power' in the*

modern World – one which dispels the notion that the individual is powerless[11]".

Robert Kennedy similarly talked of a ripple of hope:

"Each time a man stands up for an ideal or acts to improve the lives of others, or strikes out against injustice, he sends a tiny ripple of hope, and those ripples, crossing each other from a million different centres of energy, build a current which can sweep down the mightiest walls of oppression and resistance[12]."

It may strike you that 'Creative Consumerism' is just another way of talking about 'Ethical' living and to a certain extent this is true. "Ethical" has certainly become a bit of a buzz word. More and more people are talking about leading ethical lifestyles, we hear more and more debates on the radio about ethical living – the need to reduce our carbon footprint for instance. It has become a hot topic…and rightly so.

But what does ethical mean? Look it up in a dictionary and you will find descriptions like "relating to or treating of morals or ethics; moral; honourable". As such you could

---

[11] 'A Year in Green Tea and Tuks-Tuks, Rory Spowers (2010)
[12] 'Day of Affirmation Address', Robert Kennedy, University of Capetown, 6 June 1966

associate it with words and behaviour such as honest, fair, just, decent, principled and right-minded. Like 'Creative Consumerism' living ethically is about leading a lifestyle which recognises the impact we have on the world, and working to make this as positive as possible.

In a utopian world we would all love leading "ethical" lifestyles, we would abandon our cars, avoid air travel, be "responsible" consumers, be happy...but there is a big problem. The companies and organisations we criminalise and blame for the world's problems – poor labour conditions, animal cruelty, pollution and so on...many of us rely upon for our living. Too easily we forget that companies are just our own creation – not body and soul - but simply a means to organise production; a means to provide goods and services for the world to consume and a means for us to make money so that we may purchase the things we need to live.

What is a corporation? Is it a means of production or a great idea to make profits without individual responsibility?

Even if we are not actually employed by the organisations we blame for the troubles of our World we conveniently forget that one way or another many of us support them by buying their goods and services, or we may even own shares in them through our pension schemes and investments. We forget that in reality there is only really one boss in a business, and that is the customer. As a business owner I am only too aware that if I am not doing right by the customer, then my customers can fire me simply by choosing to do business elsewhere.

CHAPTER SEVEN

CREATIVE COMPANIES

"A business that makes nothing but money is a poor business."

Henry Ford

People often say that once you've lived in Norwich, UK you'll never want to leave. Maybe that's why it's called 'a fine city'; a fact proudly declared as you enter. If you happen to drive by the centre of this Fine City you may notice a building which on first glance appears to be a perfectly normal office. But if you take a closer look you will see that the floors are connected by a large slide; visible through the large glass windows. There's also a bar, a ping pong and a pool table. This is where you will find the headquarters of Naked Wines.

Naked Wines launched in 2008 with the aim of revolutionising wine sales. The strategy was simple – to make direct connections between the wine makers and their customers (known as Angels); "Our winemakers get to sell all of their wines, and make a living. We make the same margins as everyone else, and have a lot of fun along the way[13]." At the last count this relatively new creative business has changed the lives of 106 winemakers in 65 places around the world helping people with a passion for wine sell their produce and rescuing those in need, such as one winery owner who had her life turned around in just 5 hours by 2,500 Angels after her business faced ruin when vandals struck her vineyard in France.

It's not just their suppliers that are happy. Employee happiness and wellbeing is at the heart of this creative business which even offers free breakfast and fruit. There's a Naked Walking Club, a Naked Yoga Club and a dedicated sensory room so staff can take time out and unwind during the day. Every month there's even a "Free Food Friday" where the company puts on lunch for everyone, provided by local foodies or prepared by one of the teams.

Whereas the sceptics amongst us will maintain that organisations and the people within them only ever act in their own best interests – usually to make the biggest profits possible, to reward shareholders, and, of course, most

[13] www.nakedwines.co.uk, Naked Wines (2019)

importantly to pay themselves as much as possible, this is a business where there's a lot more to it than profit; and, importantly, a business that's thriving.

The other rather depressing view of the modern organisation is underpinned by mainstream economic theory. Businesses, we hear, exist only to make a profit. To spend time doing anything which detracts from this most worthy of goals is considered foolhardy – or even unjust to the companies' shareholders.

If we accept this view, the modern organisation is no more than a money-making machine. It has scant regard for anything else. It does not care for people. It does not care for our natural environment or living environment. The modern organisation cares only about making money.

This view of the modern organisation is the same view that condemns thousands of people to boring jobs and poor working conditions; it is responsible for the destruction of our natural environment, and condemns millions of people to live in poverty, whilst the minority of us have more than we can really appreciate.

If we continue to embrace this view of modern business our world will remain dominated by greedy organisations, obsessed with making short term profits and accumulating financial resources in the name of economic development and progress. With many global organisations now wealthier than entire countries, it's a sobering thought. We may elect our politicians but have little control over the head of massive organisations.

Despite having a love hate relationship with technology, I've sometimes wondered where I might find a job in this sector which is brimming with examples of creative employers as they boast top rankings in the list of the best places to work. A quick look at the perks of working in these organisations and it is easy to see why; employees are encouraged to play a key role, often within their first few weeks, workplaces provide access to great ongoing learning opportunities, to balance the daily stresses of work there's onsite access to Yoga, Pilates and Massage and there is no need to worry if you have overslept or need to go straight out after work, as restaurants serve up breakfast, lunch and dinner. It's no wonder that talented people are attracted to work in these places as they are rewarded for their contribution to the organisations' success but, perhaps more exciting, they are empowered to change the World.

No doubt providing all these perks is expensive. Yet, there is significant evidence which suggests that being a creative employer can pay dividends. Many of these companies are not just creative; they are also very successful financially.

In 1951, Ernest Bader, the founder of Scott Bader, now a global chemical company, made a choice to give up his fortune and take the company from private ownership into a structure which allowed its success to be shared with its workers. He didn't feel comfortable with the idea of amassing a personal fortune and instead wanted a way of distributing the capital of the company which was less divisive and allowed all employees to have a 'real' say in the company. Decades later and the company continues to flourish turning over €230 million globally and employing almost 700 people across 6 manufacturing sites and 13 offices. In this time Scott Bader's philosophy has always been that a business should only exist to create value for the people of our planet and it has been very successful at doing so.

Without this creative structure, perhaps the company would have still enjoyed success but it makes me wonder how much personal wealth is enough. Ernest Bader was still a relatively wealthy man – just not an extraordinarily wealthy man. Certainly, extraordinary wealth does not seem to add to our happiness with many very 'successful' entrepreneurs and business leaders reporting that they can never have enough. They always want more. Our insatiable appetites rage. I wonder when wealth changes from a reward for hard work, genius or just pure good fortune to a dangerous game where enormous power is wielded by the individual?

Investigative Journalist, Oliver Bullough published
Money Land in 2019[14]. It's a controversial story of how
the obscenely wealthy can simply bypass usual societal
rules and legislation through offshore tax havens. Perhaps
most useful is the way it illustrates a key point – there is
simply a level of wealth which is undesirable for an individual to have. Yet, focusing only on efficiency and profits
produces a small minority with billions of financial wealth
and thousands of people working all the hours God sends
to break even.

I heard Priya Lakhani speak at an investment confer-
ence in London. The aftermath of a 3-course lunch had
muted the atmosphere and it would have been easy to tune
out. Yet she captivated the room describing how, at a
young age she wanted to make a difference in the World.
She, like me, had experienced a life changing moment
when travelling abroad with her parents. Describing how
motor problems had forced her parents to make an un-
scheduled stop during a journey, she and her sister had
killed time at the roadside kicking a ball around with the
locals. She was struck by how inadequately clothed the
other children were, and after bonding over a common love
of football, was mortified when her parents drew up in the
family's white Mercedes and she and her sister were in-
structed to climb in. In that moment of embarrassment and

---

[14] 'Moneyland', Oliver Bullough (2018)

sense of undeserved privilege Priya decided that she would do something about inequality.

Years later, ignoring the doubts of her teachers, she would successfully train as a lawyer, believing that this would be a good way to make a difference in the World. Once a lawyer she turned caterer after spotting a hole in the market for pre-prepared authentic Indian foods; she felt an impossible burden to prepare the fresh Indian cooking sauces expected of her when long working hours as a lawyer meant she had no time to prepare food and cook. Therein Masala Masala was born; the mission simple to use only fresh, authentic ingredients to make cooking sauces Supermarkets could stock so that other people could prepare delicious Indian cuisine in the fraction of the normal time. But importantly she recognised this also as an opportunity to fulfil her dream to reduce inequality, declaring that for every meal sold she would pay for a meal for the underprivileged in India and Africa. By 2016 the charitable arm of Masala Masala had provided over one million meals and 35,000 vaccinations[15].

Today Priya runs Century Tech whose mission is to combine data analytics and cognitive neuroscience to help teachers provide personalised learning support. True to her promise, the company provides this free of charge to underprivileged schools.

---

[15] https://startups.co.uk/young-guns/priya-lakhani/ (2016)

Over many years the Body Shop helped keep my skin in reasonably good shape despite the stresses of childbirth, parenthood and daily life. Irrespective of this remarkable achievement, this creative company pursued a relentless quest to go beyond the business of making money. The late Dame Anita Roderick grew The Body Shop from a small independent beauty retailer in the seaside town of Brighton, England, into a massive organisation operating in countries spanning the globe. Anita famously said that "The business of business should not just be about money, it should be about responsibility. It should be about public good, not private greed[16]". And, she meant what she said - The Body Shop's history is brimming with examples of responsible behaviour. The Body Shop was the first company to bring fair trade to the beauty industry. Anita simply did not believe that it was right that her suppliers should struggle on subsistence wages whilst her business thrived. Instead, she believed in paying a fair price for their contribution to her products. In doing so she made a real difference to the lives of farmers, their families, producers and communities across the world, and The Body Shop continues to do so today through Community Trade arrangements. It is also well known for its campaigns tackling important issues including the child sex trade and violence in the home.

---

[16] Dame Anita Roderick, source unknown

Then there are unlikely heros. In the late 90s long before the days of corporate social responsibility boards and public pressure, one franchise in the fast-food sector pledged to cook only with free-range eggs. Perhaps it was caution and cynicism which kept the news out of the headlines yet over 20 years later they have remained true to their pledge. I am not suggesting that the fast-food sector is a shining example of a creativity but it's important to understand that this one decision stretched far beyond its boundaries. It had an enormous impact on the farming industry. With over ninety million eggs a year and counting consumed at this particular franchise it literally changed the lives of millions of hens. I personally would prefer to buy breakfast at a local, independent cafe where I know the food will be delicious and the eggs, free-range. But important though it's purchasing decisions are independent small businesses will never have the same influence our global brands have on food supply chains. Could you imagine what would happen if other big organisations followed suit, or if similar policies were adopted across entire menus. Imagine what kind of world we would live in if others followed suit.

And what about creative products? Here it gets really exciting. Recently we have seen developments with Seaweed and disposable packaging. Seaweed is 100% biodegradable, decomposing within four to six weeks. It's abundant too. It's estimated that, if used as packaging, just 0.03 per cent of the world's brown seaweed, could replace all of the polyethylene terephthalate (PET) plastic bottles we get through each year.

The thing is we already have this capability. One Christmas, some years ago, I received a popular box of chocolates which proudly declared that all wrappings could go in my compost bin. Sure enough the little shiny pink, blue, silver and gold wrappings broke down and have since helped nourish my garden. Yet companies still use non-compostable options because (presumably) it's cheaper or maybe it's just an easier option.

Until recently the only electric vehicles we would see on the roads were milk floats and we would all queue behind them for miles as they struggled to reach speeds of 15 mph. Anyone who's watched "Jonny English Strikes Again" will have enjoyed the moment when the baddies overtake his (admittedly dated) sports car in their gleaming electric motor. Today electric cars increasingly offer a genuine alternative to petrol and diesel options with experts working to find a genuine 'green' solution. After all, the electricity still has to be generated somehow. Who knows what type of technological breakthrough the future holds? Perhaps most exciting is the potential for hydrogen powered cars – a technology which if it can be successfully and safely developed has the potential to radically reduce the level of carbon emissions into our atmosphere. Of course, it's not going to do the environment much good if we still replace our cars every 2 or 3 years.

Lots of creative technologies have already changed our lives. In my childhood I proudly sported the latest slim line Walkman even though it meant carrying around a stack of cassette tapes and then later CDs with me. Now there is little evidence in my home that I own any music. I simply download or stream my favourite artists and tracks – there is no need to worry about adding yet another CD to my collection - I get to enjoy the music I want to listen to straightaway. What a great way to reduce our consumption habits. I don't even need a separate device anymore as my mobile phone allows me to listen to all my music, not to mention browse the web, watch TV and do my shopping.

Yet, the environmental potential of these technologies will be short lived if we do not adopt a creative approach to our hardware needs. It has never failed to surprise me how quickly new technology becomes redundant as even newer models are launched. If we want meaningful change, we need technologies which can be upgraded with new capabilities so we don't have to regularly replace them. Sadly, by taking the view that the natural world is ours to use as we please, a 'free' resource, it is too profitable for companies to be wasteful. Electronic waste is already the fastest growing form of rubbish worldwide. In 2019 the World generated 53.6 million metric tons of e-waste[17] – that's over two thirds of the weight of the moon which weighs an estimated 73.5 million metric tons[18] and with electronic waste increasing at the rate of 2.5 million metric tons each year it won't be long before we have to look for a planet to make the comparison. Worst most still ends up in landfill sites or incinerators. This is not surprising when many of us have mobile phone contracts which provide us with a new model every so many months and computers last just a few years before their technology becomes outdated. We recently had a washing machine repaired for the second time. The engineer commented that despite being over 10 years old it was still worth repairing as it should be able to last for several more years. Shame the same can't be said for newer models, he said, which are built to fail.

But what's really exciting about creative change is the potential to dream beyond our own current limited view of the World and reach beyond our own capabilities. Anyone who has been married or in a relationship long enough will tell you that there are some things there are no point arguing about. In our house it concerned a pair of pyjamas. Lovingly brought as a [useful] stocking present for my husband in the early years of our marriage this seemingly innocent pair of navy pyjamas would be the source of

---

[17] 'The Global E-Waste Monitor 2020', SCYCLE, UNU, UNITAR, ITU & ISWA (2020)
[18] https://weightofstuff.com/how-much-does-the-moon-weigh/ (2020)

conflict for years to come. My husband sniggered when I said they were navy, and would swear on his life they were black. I, on the other hand, as the proud owner then of an almost entirely black wardrobe, would swear on my life they were navy. We never agreed and eventually [thankfully] they wore out and I consigned them to the 'rag bag'. Years later we still disagree about certain colours. Perhaps one of us is a little colour blind or maybe we both are, but the point is we each see our World through our own lens and find it difficult to accept that there might be another, equally 'right' way.

These fixed ideas of viewing the World limit our imagination of what it could be. For instance, people often comment that for an economy to be successful it will always be destructive – what would happen to our investment portfolios, they worry, if companies could not trade as they do now. But we're forgetting that we still need to consume and there are many people in the World who need to consume more just to live. Writing in the midst of the Covid-19 crisis, confined to home with a once the week anxious trip to the shops, we have all been reminded how reliant we are on the economy around us. I wanted to cry when the supermarket assistant confiscated the beans and pulses from my trolley, telling me that I had exceeded my allowance. I am feeding a family of five, I wanted to shout and don't eat meat. What else should I buy. I later realised I should have gorged on Easter Eggs, there were no limits on buying them.

And then there are the things which make living worthwhile. Personally, in the days of 'lock down' I couldn't wait to go out to eat again, looking longingly at the pubs and restaurants in the tourist spot I live as I passed on my daily exercise. My daughter was bursting with excitement when her favourite musical was aired during this time. Sceptical of watching it on screen I reluctantly agreed to join her. A few hours later, the drama, music, dance and sheer amazing talent had transported us to another place and fed our souls. To say that Covid-19 will consign live music, theatre and so on to history by pessimists is to underestimate its importance in the World and deny our humanity. What's life without music, dance and theatre?

I have recently been working on a renovation project aiming to refurbish a house with a mainly recycled and up-cycled interior. However, I don't like buying furniture online as I find it difficult to judge its quality and what it really looks like from a picture. Yet, after hours of driving around rural Norfolk with my eldest daughter who I had persuaded to join me in my quest for interior design perfection, we struggled to find enough furniture to fill even the smallest room despite hours of meticulous research beforehand. In the same time that we made precisely no progress I could have walked into any one of a number of high street shops and furnished the whole house with ease with brand new products. There's no rule that says shops cannot sell second hand furniture – it's just that through our lens of the

World second hand or upcycled furniture remains the preserve of charity shops, auction houses and online retailers.
It simply doesn't feature on the so-called high street.

The same is true of so much other waste. Rather than
replace my various technologies when they stop working
properly, I would love to have them repaired. But being
useless at anything technical I need someone to provide this
service. Yet, it's either impossibly expensive that only a
fool would agree or there's no market for second hand re-
pairs. What about clothes. It's no secret in our house that
I hate sewing. I always seem to be able to jab the needle
into different parts of my body and my best efforts look like
the work of a five-year-old. Yet, the ability to repair
clothes easily would reduce the amount of clothes which
are thrown away unnecessarily. What's to say that someone couldn't set up a business to upcycle clothes in the
same way that we can upcycle furniture. I'd rush to shop
somewhere that sold this type of range, finding it impossible to find the time or inclination to source good clothes in
charity shops.

An annual Spa trip has been one of the highlights of my
year over the last fifteen years, as my best friend and I take
some time away from the stresses of modern-day life. We
could qualify as professional critics as our travels have
taken us around our local area and beyond in the quest for
Spa perfection. It was always a tall order to beat our first
experience. This featured inclusive yoga sessions, where

the lady in front trumped aloud to the background music and I was almost kicked out for giggling; a wonderful massage which I loved but my friend hated and in her haste to leave the treatment room forgot that her feet were covered in oil leaving her sprawled, semi naked on the floor; and the facial which I fell asleep in, only to face an entire waiting room of people when I had to be woken up. There are many experiences and services, which if approached creatively, need not be destructive. A spa, for example, can be incredibly wasteful, use hundreds of towels every day and require a ton of carbon to heat, or it could aim to be sustainable, use natural products, encourage guests to bring their own towels and use renewable energy supplies. Some years ago we holidayed at Lake Garda in Northern Italy where we had the choice of two water parks; one boasting some of the largest slides in Europe, colourful and concrete and, frankly, very tempting, another, our eventual choice, a water park landscaped into its natural environment with rock, sand and hundreds of plants dividing up the different pools and slides, and, importantly using natural alternatives to the harsh chemicals usually deployed to keep swimming pools clean. It was a beautiful and inspiring place to visit and I left without a trace of chorine on my body and feeling truly alive.

Who's to say that with a little imagination and recognition of the important things in life we couldn't have more businesses that do offer genuinely environmentally friendly goods and services, and importantly, businesses which prosper. Businesses which are good both for the people they serve and the people who serve within them, and, not least, the World on which they rely so heavily.

CHAPTER EIGHT

A CHANGE OF HEART

We have robbed the younger generation of their future. Or rather that's what recent reports would have us believe as thousands of young people demonstrate against climate change. When interviewed Arlie, a 17-year-old from Birmingham claimed that "Anyone who has been on the planet longer than us; they have been irresponsible. They have been irresponsible in their actions and their attitude towards the climate."

My eldest was staggered when I refused to allow her to take a day off school to participate in the recent protests; "I thought you cared about the environment!" she complained. I love the thought that she was motivated by a deep desire for change but suspect the idea of a day off school and trip to London was the main attraction. Telling her that I may reconsider (a lie I admit) if she actually bothered to put the recycling in the recycling bin and the compost in the compost bin did not improve matters - I often feel like it's me versus the rest of my family as I constantly pick the cardboard and apple cores out of the general waste and reallocate them to the correct bins. Then my mum joined-in. Not usually inclined to side with me I was surprised as she proceeded to lecture my daughter about her childhood and how dare she stand accused of "ruining the World"; her generation, she exclaimed, were far less wasteful than yours'. Contrasting her life with my daughter's she then recounted how she walked the mile and a half to school each day, rather than getting a ride in a bus; how she played with her friends in the street rather than getting a lift to numerous clubs and extra-circular activities. Holidays aboard, "you must be joking! One week in a caravan at Walton-on-the-Naze was the highlight of my childhood." At this point I could see my daughter mentally trying to work out how many foreign holidays she's been on whilst feigning interest. "Supermarket shopping" my mum continued "for all those handy ready meals and pizzas. Never! I walked to the shops and then carried the heavy bags home; no wonder I was a size 10 then, who needs a gym membership?" Apparently at the tender age of 12 she graduated to a Wicker Trolley Basket on wheels. I chuckled knowing that my daughter wouldn't be seen dead wheeling a wicker shopping basket. Next came plastic. I sensed that this was all getting a bit much. First on the list was drinks – and not the alcoholic variety. Bottled water, my mum explained, did not exist when she was young. It came from a tap, if indoors. Parks and schools had public fountains and everyone used them. Milk came in bottles, usually delivered to her door 6 days a week by a milkman with an electric float. As a real treat there were a few fizzy drinks. Her mum, my Grandma kept a supply of Tizer and Cream Soda; they were favourites and were usually bought at a local shop. They came in glass bottles for which you paid a few pence deposit, which was refunded when bottles were returned. Apparently for luckier kids the "Corona Man" delivered a fortnightly supply of pop, but again all these came in refundable glass bottles. Fruit and Veg came from a greengrocer, who weighed what you wanted and put them in a brown paper bag. Meat was bought at the Butchers, weighed, then wrapped in paper. Newspapers were delivered by paperboys on bikes. When read, they were used to light fires, wrap rubbish or provide padding when packing. I thought then to intervene thinking that there is only so much that a teenager can take on board, but now on a roll nothing could stop my mum as she moved on to the use of electricity and disposables. First came nappies. My eldest was amazed that disposable nappies were not a thing. In my mum's day, nappies were terry toweling squares, with plastic pants on top. These were soaked in a solution in a bucket, then washed and hung out to dry. There were no automatic washing machines or tumble dryers. The best you could expect was a twin-tub and a spin dryer, then if it was warm (and you were lucky), they dried outside but if it rained you had to rely on the wooden horse in front of the fire. No wonder that then most children were potty trained by 2 compared to the many children today who remain in nappies until their early school years.

Not much was disposable. No biro's; they wrote with a fountain pen filled with real ink. Razors were stainless steel and only the blades were changed regularly. The list was endless. My daughter, now totally tuned out smiled sweetly saying "Thanks Grandma. You've really made me think about things" but my mum wasn't going to let her get away quite so easily "So, what do you think of my generations' 'Green-ness now?"

The thing is like my children many young people don't realise the massive shift we have seen in material consumption and how much has changed in a relatively short space of time. Even in my childhood I didn't travel by air. I was 20 when I travelled by plane for the first time, nervously gripping my fiancée's hand, my sweaty palm betraying my fear. And how ironic that our young people are so unhappy when for many people, working to provide for their children has been one of their main motivations, and whilst there is a great deal of inequality, as my mum lectured, many children today enjoy lifestyles that their parents could have only dreamt of.

I admit that I am a natural optimist. I can find the positive in most difficult circumstances even managing to convince myself that being admitted to hospital for a weekend rather than attending a friends' Wedding was a great opportunity to catch up on my professional development. But the trouble with a lot of discussion about the challenges of climate change is that young people seem to feel totally overwhelmed by it, and rather than motivated to bring about change in the World, are struggling to visualise their future, even to the point that they don't, in fact, see the point of trying. This is troubling. We should be focusing on educating and working with young people to motivate them to be the change they want to see in the World; to challenge existing patterns of thinking without simply pointing the finger of blame or joining in protests, which whilst some serve a purpose, others are simply an excuse for vandalism.

Contrary to my 'glass half full' mentality, Covid-19 has brought the pessimists out in abundance and given them an international stage. The pandemic has inflicted difficulties, hardship and pain on many people and we are not out of the woods yet. However, there have also been a great many good things too. We've seen communities come together in ways not seen since the War, people have displayed great acts of kindness and dedication to their profession, with many making massive sacrifices to maintain and provide healthcare, to support the vulnerable and protect the sick to name just a few. We've seen companies show great resilience and adapt. I've lost track of the number of different policies and processes we've adopted and changed in my company; at the onset of Covid-19 the ink hadn't even dried on our latest crisis plan before we had to write another. My team have been amazing, resilient and quick to change, and so have so many others. Yet, we still fixate on the negative.

Psychologists agree that we are wired for negativity reporting that humans tend to remember traumatic experiences better than positive ones, respond more strongly to negative things than positive ones and remember insults far more readily than praise. This negative bias means that we pay much more attention to the bad things that happen, which makes them feel much more important than they really are. Nowhere is this illustrated more clearly than the media, where sadness, trauma, theft, death, disease and tragedy dominate, with good news often relegated. Yet we have much to be pleased about. I wrote earlier that we still need economic growth, just a different kind to the type we have been conditioned to need.

Historically nothing has worked better than economic growth in enabling societies to improve the life changes of their members, including those at the very bottom.[19]

Growth helps people move away from Poverty, it enables them to reach their potential and follow their talents,

[19] Dani Rodrik, Harvard University, One Economics, Many Recipes: Globalization, Institutions and Economic Growth (2007)

and the right type of growth can help us overcome the challenges we face in the World. The advancements and improvements we have seen in the World in the last 50 years are undeniable; people are living longer than ever before, there's better access to healthcare, new treatments mean that previous death sentences have been commuted, to name just a few. The main 'loser' is the environment, and it's the environment to which our attention must now be drawn.

As yet there are no Trillionaires in the World but each of us can boast that we have over 100 Trillion neural connections, or synapses, in our brains. These connections transfer electric activity (information) from one cell to another. Researchers have found that the ability of the brain to transmit and process information requires a lifelong commitment to maintaining the integrity of our synapses. The thing is, it is also very difficult to 'un-program' these connections.

This probably explains why when faced with everyday decisions, such as what to eat, what food to buy, how to spend our free time we tend to fall back into comfortable routines and can easily become stuck in a rut. For many years I wanted to eat less meat prompted by the environmental benefits and a general preference for alternatives, until eventually I realised that the only way to climb out of the rut I had found myself in was to go 'cold turkey' and give it up completely. It was one of the best decisions I ever made – and I have never missed it in my diet substituting it with alternatives I much prefer and enjoy.

Another time life had been particularly challenging; there was no specific catastrophe, but I felt worn down by its relentless pace and was really looking forward to having some time off for some of the things which were really important for me and, frankly, some peace and quiet.

The problem was that when the opportunity to have some free time finally arose, somehow, I just didn't feel like doing anything much. So rather than doing some of the things I love or wanted to get done I just sat around feeling increasingly dissatisfied and grumpy. And as the minutes ticked by, my frustration grew; here was the time I had been really looking forward to, and rather than pursuing the things that I enjoyed or were important to me I was fed up. It was as though my brain, unused to less pressure, had malfunctioned and I just couldn't get into doing anything.

Mel Robbins, international author and motivational speaker, talks about change in her international best-selling book, "The 5 Second Rule[20]". When reading Mel's book, I realised that we all struggle with the same underlying issues. We get stuck in our own ruts. One part of our mind may be secretly begging us to change, whilst another is

---

[20] "The 5 Second Rule", Mel Robbins (2017)

scared to change and tries to talk us out of it. I started running at the beginning of the Covid-19 crisis in a bid to maintain my fitness and balance the massive challenges I faced in my business. Every morning I battled with the demons in my head which told me I couldn't do it; surely, they said, I would fail, be run over in the dark lanes around my home or worse, abducted and murdered. Mel's book got me through it. More, it made me realise that, despite years passing since my Dad's sudden death, I was still finding it hard to get the things done which were really important to me. It was as if I still believed that another day in the future, I would have an amazing epiphany and find a miraculous way to change. I was wrong. There was no simple solution. Somehow, we each have to find our own way in the World, and make time for the things that we really important to us. Mel's book is a must for anyone who wants to achieve meaningful change in their life. And with the trillions of neural connections we each boast in our brains we basically need to reprogram our brains if we want to change; and change we must.

"Infinite growth of material consumption in a finite world is an impossibility."

E F Schumacher

Whatever you believe about global warming one thing is certain; our planet cannot support endless material consumption. This gives us a choice. We can continue our pursuit of happiness in all things material, irrespective of how successful the outcome - all the time doing our best to be blissfully unaware of the cliff edge we race towards - or we can value what is really important to us, and to support our values, and hopefully by doing so work towards a better world.

> *"We humans have been very good at creating problems – but we can be equally good at solving them...a sustainable world is not an unachievable goal. As the world looks to restore its economies we must build in long-term environmental as well as economic sustainability."*

David Norman, Director of Campaigns at WWF-UK

So if we value fresh air, we should value it when we are choosing whether to drive to the shops or take the 'park and ride'; if we value our natural environment, we should value it when we decide what we consume; if we value our oceans, we should eliminate the waste that's likely to end up in them and so on.

Of course, no-one wants to read a long list of what they should and should not buy or consume...after all, we all have different values and we don't want to become en-trapped by a new brand of consumer 'police' by those who like nothing more than to cast judgement on others. Liter-ally hundreds of people flocked to enjoy the river and riverside pubs in the tourist village I live as the first Covid-19 lockdown slowly lifted, watched over by local residents; some rightly cross about the many badly parked cars and boy racers, others counting the groups of people and de-claring them 'illegal' secretly delighted at the excuse to have a rant on social media. Yet it's important that we un-derstand that the way we behave shapes the world around us.

Few can deny that we need to reduce the amount of car-bon dioxide emitted into our atmosphere to have a hope of keeping climate change at bay. Experts advise that a fifty percent reduction is required by 2050 with as much as an eighty percent reduction required in industrialised coun-tries to avoid 'climate chaos'.

It is going to take more than a few of us walking our children to school or taking the bus to work to achieve these targets. We need an energy revolution. We need to funda-mentally change the way we generate energy and we need to fundamentally change the way we live and work. And we all need to start doing it now. We cannot leave it to 'someone else', as the chances are that 'someone else' is leaving it to us. We need to remember that individual choices play a key role, particularly concerning transport, diet and housing, and international agreements alone will not stop climate change. The good news is that scientists and engineers agree that we already have the technology and capability to make industry work without compromising the planet. So, what can we do?

First and foremost, we need to start with ourselves. We need to consider our lifestyles, home and our habits and ask whether these are really in line with our values and what's important to us; are they what we really want from life? Perhaps one of the hardest challenges we've explored is that often it's not the things we do or consume that make us happy, it's the people we do them with, the shared experiences and the sheer knowledge of feeling that you belong, that someone cares about you. As a family we often holiday in France, breaking up the drive with an overnight stay in a bed and breakfast. One trip took us to the Loire valley, stopping at fabulous farmhouse where we enjoyed a four-course meal with our hosts produced from the fruits of their labour in the surrounding acres. That night however, we were awoken by our youngest who was then just a year old, a high temperate indicating that all was not well. Locating the emergency medicine, like all good parents we pack religiously, she eventually fell asleep. Sadly, for the next week though, sleep would evade her as she fought the germs that consumed her body with the result that the family in the tent next to ours at the pretty French campsite positively hated us. Worse, the same family seemed to have befriended all the other Brits visiting the site, but when we emerged from our tent worn out from a relentless quest to keep our little girl quiet animosity positively leaked out of them and I began to suspect they had told everyone to ignore us. It was a far cry from our experience the following year, befriending our neighbours when camping in Lake Garda. Days and nights disappeared in a flurry of drinks, shared meals and chats as we got to know each other. In the same way in the midst of the Covid-19 crisis, the challenges of being confined to our homes were undeniable, but many of the people I have spoken to reported that they felt somehow better for the opportunity to reconnect with their friends and family in a way that they never seemed to have time for before.

If we really value our world, then we should start by saving energy in our homes. A few wise buying decisions and a change of wasteful habits, and you can soon reduce the amount of energy you consume (and cut your household bills). It may be lighting, it may be heating, it may be cooking, it may be your old fridge which consumes over twice the energy of a good quality modern one – it may be insulation, it may be something else, but whatever it is we need to actually read the plethora of advice increasingly provided by our energy companies, our councils and so on, and cut our energy consumption.

A lot of this starts with our buying decisions. I have always thought that it is a crazy idea to rate the efficiency of domestic appliances and then give people the choice to purchase one that is so inefficient you could probably fly half way around the World and back every few years for the amount of extra energy it is consuming.

Despite being available for many years, it is only in recent years that the purchase of 'old style' light bulbs in the European Union have been outlawed in favour of more energy efficient models. I remember listening with dismay as I heard a caller tell a popular radio show how he had purchased all the supplies of 'old style' bulbs he could find so that he need never switch to the more efficient model. The interesting thing is that as the old style became outlawed, the choice and quality of energy efficient lighting rocketed. It's now possible to buy bulbs which will last for years which use just a fraction of the energy of their predecessors and, notably, don't take an age to light up.

Culture plays a big role. I have "A Fantastic Bag". It is made from recycled plastic drinks bottles and folds up neatly in my handbag waiting for its moment of glory when it is unfolded and loaded up. Like fairly-traded goods and free-range eggs, the idea of taking our own bags to the shops is hardly revolutionary, but we have seen a phenomenal change in recent years. Having disliked the traditional plastic disposable shopping bags for many years now, I have always been fond of reusables. But until a handful of years ago I was in the minority. I would insist on packing my shopping into my own bags – often to deaf ears as shop assistants helpfully tried to pack up for me – and walk to my car dismayed as everyone buzzed around me with trolleys laden with disposable bags. Occasionally I would see a fellow reusable bag lover and smile at the knowledge that I was not on my own. Now, with the introduction of a small charge for plastic bags in a relatively short space of time we have seen a dramatic shift with the majority of people shunning the disposable version for their own bags. Now if I forget my own bags, I find myself leaving the shop as quickly as possible glancing around guiltily for fear of other peoples' disapproval. Yet we still fill our shopping trolleys with goods and packaging that is terribly wasteful and cannot be recycled.

Rightly, single use plastics have finally come under the radar, helped by various documentaries bringing home a bleak reality. My colleagues recently returned from a holiday in Thailand. I envisioned scenes of beautiful beaches, cocktails and glorious sunsets. Instead they were saddened, explaining that in one resort, hotel staff would get up early each morning to clear the beach of the mountains of waste which had been washed up from the night before. It was a sobering reality.

I had a meeting at a large insurance company recently. We met in the on-site café and when offered a drink, I asked for a cup of tea. Apologetically the organiser explained that I could only have a hot drink if I had brought a cup with me. The company had recently introduced a ban on single use plastic, so if you wanted a drink you had to provide a cup. Whilst I would have dearly loved a cup of tea, this bold move will save tons of waste from landfill given that this particular company employ over 30,000 people.

Yet many businesses are still so wasteful. In my profession I regularly attend conferences packed with cheap freebies ironically often from companies professing to offer the latest in 'socially responsible' investment solutions. Worse, people leave with bags laden with them; pens, and diaries, toys and power chargers, drinks bottles and key rings to name a few. I saw one man with two large freebie bags filled to the brim. What was he planning to do with it, I wondered; sell it on E-bay?

When my eldest was young people thought I was a wicked mum because when frequenting a certain fast-food restaurant, I used to discretely ask staff not to include whatever 'free' toy which accompanied the children's meal. Admittedly there were some tricky questions to answer as my children got older, and I didn't always get away with it, but let's face it who wants or indeed needs another bit of cheap and nasty plastic, or less than adorable cuddly toy in their life? As my children have got older, I have explained to them why I don't like this type of 'gift' and generally I think they understand. I like to think that they will pass it onto their children. I'm hoping that I won't be remembered as the mum who was so mean that they were not allowed to have the freebies, but the mum who had the common sense to understand that some freebies are simply not worth having.

And it doesn't end with freebies or children's meals; it is the badges and medals we receive or buy in the name of charity; it is the cheap and nasty cuddly toys that arrive on Valentine's Day; it is the contents of the party bags that our children bring home from friends' birthdays. It's the fact that in many supermarkets its virtually impossible to buy fruit and vegetables which are not encased in plastic tubs and wrappers.

What about children's toys? I simply do not understand why children need so many often poorly made toys. Ask most parents and I bet their children play with just a small fraction of their toys, yet, as a society, we still think the best way to show a child we love them is to buy them stuff. It's well researched that our happiness or satisfaction is not proportionate to the number of things we have. I've watched my children open a stack of presents at birthdays or Christmas, and after a point, their eyes glaze over, and gifts are quickly disregarded. Once my daughter begged us to buy her the latest craze – a fidget spinner – a little toy that spins in your hand. She said it was all she ever wanted. How long did it last? The answer - less than a week. No one knows exactly how many have been sold but toy analysts estimate that at least 19m were sold in the 12 rich-world countries during the first six months of 2017. Others put the figure at over 50m. I wonder how many and how quickly these toys made their way to landfill sites because one thing is certain – they are not very easy to recycle.

Joseph Schumpeter, an Austrian economist and later a Harvard professor, coined the phrase 'Creative Destruction' to describe the process by which seemingly unknown or new businesses can overtake established industry leaders through innovation. Few young people today will recognise the brand IBM. When I quizzed my teenager what she thought it stood for she guessed 'International Balance Magazine.' Imagine her surprise when I explained how when I was her age, they were one of the largest computer companies in the World. Yet, they failed to recognise how easily rival firms could develop their own computer hardware, ignoring the massive business opportunity represented by developing a compatible operating system. Signing a contract in 1980 with Microsoft to develop the operating system, they had little idea that Microsoft would later become the largest IT company in the world, and its founder, one of the richest people in it.

The exciting thing is that we can use the process of Creative Destruction to our own advantage. Simply by changing our buying habits companies will get the message that we do not want them to literally cost us the world because they have a horribly inefficient or wasteful way of providing us with goods and services, or produce goods of dubious quality. By supporting creative companies and buying creative products we can tell the market that we want companies that adopt the latest technology and work hard to deliver extraordinarily brilliant products. Likewise, by supporting creative organisations we can tell the market that we do not want companies that are interested in nothing more than their profit margin. We want companies who care about their natural World, their living World and their employees. If more of us shunned inefficient and environmentally wasteful products in favour of greener models or greener options, like we've seen with lightbulbs, companies would be falling over themselves to bring us more efficient models and new technologies. Innovation would prevail.

"You must be the change you wish to see in the world."

Mohandas Gandhi

As the light was failing one early autumn evening my youngest daughter was subjected to a harrowing ordeal. I'm not particularly fond of worms but as a keen gardener we have learnt a mutual respect. I try not to disturb them too much or accidently sever them in two with my spade, if they can avoid slithering over my hand when I'm not paying attention. However, our understanding does not extend to the compost bin. They love to fill it, particularly the lid, gleefully munching on the contents I empty each week from the kitchen caddy. No-one else in my family will do it, especially not my husband – he puts it in the normal bin when he thinks I'm not looking. The result is that if I am away on business for a few days it's not uncommon that I return to find the bin overflowing. The lecture I gave my family on this particularly occasion must have been quite effective as I suddenly had, not one but two young helpers. If only the older helper had listened when I warned her to be careful with the lid, adding that there were literally hundreds of worms squished under it; "What" she exclaimed turning to hold it above the youngest's head spraying her with tiny creatures in the process. As I removed hundreds of worms and maggots from her hair and body, I reminded myself that the compost bin is a great way to reduce the amount of waste we send to landfill, improves soil quality and helps water drainage, it can eliminate waste removal with estimates that in some countries up to 50% of waste sent to landfill is compostable. Not to mention the fact that it reduces the need for artificial pesticides and fertilisers. If, like plastic shopping bags, people were no longer able to send organic waste to landfill, there would be a compost revolution, so why not give it a go. And if you're finding it hard to get the motivation, read Mel's 5 Second Rule first.

Without doubt, advances in technology have fundamentally changed our lives. Twenty years ago, few would have thought that at the touch of a screen you could browse and order any number of products to be delivered the next day.

The first mobile phone I owned took ages just to send a text message. The problem is, whilst technological change can deliver great societal benefits and is an essential tool for our future, it's too easy to forget what is really important to us, what makes us truly human.

My husband brought me a smart watch for a recent birthday. It's great to be able to track the steps I take during the day, and keep an eye on how hard I am working out at the gym, but I soon realised how addictive it is. Mine is programmed to congratulate me when I reach 10,000 steps in a day (if you can call vibrating on my wrist and sending the digital equivalent of fireworks into the air as congratulations – personally I would prefer a glass of prosecco). It was at around 9,800 steps one day that I was ready for bed. The problem was that in the back of my mind I only had another 200 steps to go. So, I couldn't help myself pacing around my bedroom – even resorting to running on the spot – to reach my target before I allowed myself to stop. How ridiculous. Without doubt I should have gone straight to bed. In fact, it doesn't take a genius to work out that exercising just before sleep is a bad idea. I couldn't even get to sleep once I had reached my goal. Yes, I was 'successful' as I reached my target but was I happy? No.

In today's monetised economy it's easy to become fixated on price. The challenge is not to become stingy. Whilst my colleagues may have nicknamed me Scrooge for my dislike of Christmas, I hope that this is a light hearted dig at my distain for Christmas jumpers and not a true reflection of my character. Afterall, who would want to be associated with the Victorian miser who thought he was gaining the World but in fact almost lost everything that was truly important to him – he just didn't realise it. It's too easy to display scrooge-like tendencies under the guise of saving money and it's important to understand the difference between good money management and stinginess.

I love working with people from all walks of life. One client, a publican, recounted a disagreement he'd had with a group of walkers the night before. They had come into his pub and asked for four glasses of tap water and a lime soda. When charged over a pound for the lime soda one complained saying that he was being ripped off because his lime cordial only cost a matter of pence. An argument ensued as the landlord pointed out that he had to provide a clean glass to drink from, someone to serve it and maintain the facilities and that he had a good mind to charge for the water too since no-one seemed very inclined to purchase anything else. I think you can imagine how the conversation went from there. The walkers may have thought they had a point, but really, they were being stingy.

In the early days of my career I worked with a couple who were so reluctant to spend money that they each had a pay-as-you-go mobile I had to call at a specific time because they would not pay for a landline or outgoing calls. Another wealthy couple recounted how they had finally decided to take some of my advice and spend some money, in this case on a new kitchen. We're so pleased with it, they exclaimed. Why, it transpired, because they had negotiated the price so low that the supplier complained that it was hardly worth the sale. The problem is that money moves in cycles creating wealth as it goes. Stinginess does the opposite. It impoverishes. People deserve to be paid for the work they do and whilst no one likes to be ripped off we need to be careful not to rip off the seller, screwing them down to the last penny just because we know they really need the business.

Fixating on cost sometimes means that we can know the price of everything and the value of nothing. What may feel like a prudent choice to economise can undermine what we are trying to achieve and actually cost more in the long term. Once asked to review a portfolio that had performed poorly over many years, I asked the clients why they hadn't made any changes before. Because we don't understand it and we didn't want to pay a professional who does. The loser was clear. Good professional advice would have provided tens of thousands of pounds return to the client after the usual fees. Instead they had nothing to show for it but regret – and a financial crisis that I was then tasked with sorting out for them. Other times we fill our houses with cheap furniture and clothes, tempted by their price tag, only to find they last a fraction of the time of better-quality alternatives. Now, I have learnt to only buy things I love and look at the price tag second. I am sure I spend less money as my purchases pass the test of time – sometimes, admittedly, to my annoyance as I would like an excuse to replace them. If you are not sure what to do to 'do your bit' for the environment get some advice – there is loads of it available – and most of it is free.

CHAPTER NINE

A JOURNEY OUT OF POVERTY

"Poverty is the only load which is the heavier the more loved ones there are to assist in bearing it."

Jean-Paul

It had been dark for nine long months but with Uzuri's growing consciousness she had felt warm and secure, comforted in the depth of her mother's womb. But now something was terribly wrong. After a brief sensation of light and an awareness of her mother's touch a new darkness had descended. A cold and suffocating darkness; it felt like it was slowing squeezing the life out of her little body. The only reaction she knew was to cry, but as her mouth filled with grit she soon learnt to stay quiet.

Uzuri means beauty; but this little beauty faced a dreadful fate. Born in one of the poorest regions of Africa she had been buried alive by her mother, who simply couldn't cope. Her rescuers don't know how long she spent in the ground but months later Uzuri remains traumatized by her ordeal. Terrified to sleep, when exhaustion finally takes hold after a brief rest Uzuri is awoken by her trembling body as she relives the nightmares in her head.

It is an uncomfortable truth that whilst some of us live in relative luxury, many more live in abject poverty. If one thing is certain; the pursuit of economic growth has provided many of us with more material wealth than our ancestors would have ever believed. Yet, despite continued improvements in recent years billions of people still struggle to survive.

In Tanzania, two little girls are crying with hunger. They are fortunate enough to cross paths with Westerners who give them the cereals bars planned for their own lunch. The little girls eat them hungrily then lick the paper. There is the young boy suffering from Malaria whose parents cannot afford the £1.50 lifesaving medication. The little albino girl in desperate need of sunscreen to protect her from the Sun's inescapable rays – her parents can only afford enough for her face; so many things that so many of us take for granted.

In this part of Tanzania many children have just one parent or none at all; some have died; some have gone away. Many young children care for younger ones and carry them around on their backs. What a contrast to modern day parenthood in the West where our children are in danger of being over protected, over fed and have far more than they can appreciate. In Tanzania a little boy plays with his model aeroplane fashioned from a wide leaf with a hole in it and a stalk pushed through it. In the UK two children are arguing over their toys. Both want to play with the model airport complete with planes, vehicles and model people and neither want to share. The argument soon moves onto the playfarm, then the trainset. In desperation their mother sends them to play in the garden where the push-bikes cause another fight.

In Tanzania many families have no work. In the UK some people choose not to work, finding it easier to live off the State. In Tanzania some families are fortunate enough to have a small plot of land to grow a few crops. Some may even be able to buy and sell their produce at the local market. In the UK we enjoy the flowers in our gardens and may grow fruit and vegetables but the thought of relying on them for food would terrify us.

Tanzanian children fortunate enough to attend school share classrooms with over sixty children and four or five children sharing a desk. There is no electricity and no modern technology; a stark contrast to Western schools.

Children, desperate to receive an education, walk up to one and a half hours a day each way just to get to school. In 'wealthy' countries many children regularly play truant and we drive them to and from school – sometimes just a matter of meters. In Tanzania children want to learn. Many have ambitions to be teachers, doctors, lawyers and so on. Joel is one of the top law students in the country, thanks to the sponsorship which gained him a place at school. Others are not so lucky.

In some ways Tanzanian children are fortunate as life is worse elsewhere. The moments after my children were born were amongst the most precious of my life. It's inconceivable that not so many miles away ten times the number of babies born in the UK every day die from the effects of poverty. I love watching my children play with their friends in the school playground. Global deaths of children under 5 years old if contained to the UK would empty the playground of every infant school[21].

We think World poverty is beyond help yet many of deaths are from preventable causes such as diarrhoea. Perhaps this is not surprising when water problems affect over half of humanity. It is so easy to take water for granted. We easily waste it because it is cheap and convenient. I have tried and I fear failed to teach my children how

---

[21] https://data.unicef.org/topic/child-survival/under-five-mortality/ (2019)

precious water is. Leaving the taps running means nothing to them. I guess I should not be surprised; my dad used to regularly lecture us about not wasting water – partly by a desire to economise and partly because he cared about the environment. It was a particularly tense time in our house when in my teens I enjoyed a long hot shower every morning – not helped by the fact that I had to walk through my parents' bedroom first. I still enjoy a hot shower every morning and try not to think of the billion plus people who at best have indirect access to water. It's frightening that we use more water flushing toilets than entire families have to share in a day.

In the same way we take our food for granted and throw it away or spend hours trying to convince our children and grandchildren to eat their dinner whilst over one in four children in developing countries are estimated to be underweight or stunted.

We constantly use and rely on electricity – even a short power cut will see us stuck for what to do. Yet a quarter of humanity live without electricity.

We overwhelm our surgeries and hospitals with minor complaints whilst every year there are hundreds of millions of cases of malaria with countless fatalities, mainly in Africa, and precious little access to medical advice and expertise.

Whilst these are terrible problems it's easy to understand how we can remove ourselves from them or feel that they are way beyond our influence. But we all play a crucial part. We help determine inequalities in the food we eat, the clothes we wear, the cars we drive and the lifestyles we lead.

We think that it isn't our fault that other people are starving yet we happily consume fish from companies which exploit natural economies and destroy local industries. Petri is a traditional fisherman. His father taught him to fish, and his grandfather taught his father. For generations families in his small fishing village have lived in harmony with the ocean, feeding themselves and their families with the produce of their catch. Today the horizon is blighted with huge trawler vessels; their expansive nets indiscriminately emptying the seas. Petri still goes out to fish but returns disappointed as local fish stocks have been wiped out. Now, his family are starving. He can only look with sadness at the sorry remains of the fish which have been caught and discarded, unwanted, by the huge trawlers as they are washed up on the shore.

We think we do not harm people living in poverty overseas yet we are the main contributors to global warming;

"..you are causing aggression to us by causing global warming...Alaska will probably become good

for agriculture, Liberia will probably become good for agriculture, but where does that leave Africa"

President Musevenil (President of Uganda)

We think we would never exploit the poor yet we support companies that do.

Even some of our most innocent actions – actions which could be beneficial for a 'poorer' country – are often to blame. Many of us Brits holiday abroad encouraged by the unpredictable and turbulent British climate. One August, instead of buying new sandals I bought a raincoat. Whilst many countries benefit from foreign visitors – especially those attracting us with their outstanding mountain ranges and lush tropical beaches - tourism can be a dangerous game to play.

Hidden behind the luxury of many holiday resorts is an ugly reality. In some countries luxury hotel resorts, surrounded by tall perimeter walls and armed security guards, deprive local people of safe water supplies – often to maintain otherwise untenable golf courses. Travel Representatives advise you not to travel beyond the confines of your hotel alone for 'safety' reasons. This is hardly surprising. If someone's luxury holiday meant that your children were denied access to safe drinking supplies, or you had to walk miles for an alternative source, wouldn't you have something to say about it. Wouldn't you be angry, and rightly so.

What about architecturally stunning resorts like Dubai. Perhaps most famous are its man-made islands. 'The World' consists of three hundred islands in the shape of the world visible from space, whilst the 'Palm Jumeirah' islands take the shape of a palm tree. Meanwhile its hotels include some of its most iconic symbols boasting new standards of excellence in Arabian hospitality. Dubai's impressive array of buildings and first-class entertainment facilities demand praise. Yet it seems that Dubai's workers are kept well away from its resorts – for fear of spoiling the landscape. Instead living in conditions far removed from luxury and working long unsocial hours away from their families.

The appeal of an all-inclusive holiday is not difficult to understand. Many of us like the idea of paying one price to enjoy as much food and drink we can consume – and often more. Sadly, too often, our money lines the pockets of large companies and bypasses the local community who have given us access to their beautiful country, allowed us to pollute their beaches and use their water, and then struggle to retain just a tiny fraction of our spending. It struck me once on this type of holiday that no-one was tipping the bar staff – yet in this line of work tips usually make up for a significant proportion of earnings. Perhaps it was no wonder that some staff looked like they would rather throw the drink in your face than pour it into a glass. And these issues, as we shall see, are really only the tip of the iceberg. Too often we let powerful markets dictate the quality of peoples' lives refusing to take responsibility for the way we are shaping other people's lives.

According to ancient Buddhist teachings, the Noble Eightfold Path sets out eight principles, which together set out how to achieve the end of suffering. One of these is 'Right Livelihood'. The Buddhist sees the function of work as a means for man to 'utilise and develop [his] faculties, to enable him to overcome his ego centeredness by joining with other people in a common task, and to bring forth goods and services needed for a becoming existence[22].' An interesting contrast to the modern economic view that work is a necessary evil, an item of cost, to be reduced and eliminated where possible leaving us 'free' to pursue our own ambitions. The trouble is that so often this misses the point and fails to recognise the importance of work in our World. Putting this thought aside for a moment perhaps that explains why foreign aid often focuses on throwing money at problems rather than looking at the real underlying issues. Economist, E E Schumacher famously wrote 'When we give a man a fish, we give him and his family a meal. When we give him a rod, we give him a capacity to catch fish, for several meals. When we give him training in how to make rods and start a business, we

---

[22] "Small is Beautiful", E E Schumacher (1973)

give him a capacity for an expanded way of life and living[23].'

Perhaps, by giving money here and there to charitable causes we are merely cutting back the weeds in a desperate attempt to get them under control when we should be pulling out the roots. Worse, we fail to realise that we are the ones who have been tending to the roots of inequality in the first place; we have let them flourish in our relentless pursuit of goods and services which has seen companies seek to reduce costs by whatever it takes, failing to consider the moral obligation of employment. We have let them grow by the type of products we buy in our shops and we have let them prosper at the hands of powerful markets and systems by considering nothing other than our own enjoyment.

Yet, despite the flaws of being human, I believe most people have good intentions at heart. I think most of us deep down are actually disappointed with our contribution to the World. If we are honest I think most of us feel uneasy that we cannot fit all our clothes in our wardrobes when so many are living with so little; that we may be struggling with our weight when other people are starving and that we are responsible for the abuse we inflict on our environment.

---

[23] "Small is Beautiful", E E Schumacher (1973)

I simply do not accept that most of us are happy to treat other people in this way. Look at the amazing efforts people go to for charity. National appeals raise tens of millions of pounds and thousands participate; hardly the action of people who could not care less. In the days after the devastating Earthquake in Haiti schools, charities, churches and businesses across the World did their best to give to the relief effort. In the UK everyday cars and Lorries scramble to squeeze out of the way of oncoming ambulances; hardly the actions of people who don't care. And today, as the Coronavirus has swept across our Nations, thousands of people have put their lives on the line to treat the sick and look after the vulnerable and the elderly.

So, if we mean well, what will it take for us to change?

CHAPTER TEN

SMALL REALLY IS BEAUTIFUL

"Man is small, and, therefore, small is beautiful[24]"

E E Schumacher

"Quack." There is a short pause before the next sound is emitted from the small plastic toy. Who would imagine that such a small object would be capable of disturbing the peace and ending what had been a relaxing, enjoyable afternoon? It never helps to be in the confines of the family car, less still when all my concentration is required to steer the car; the rain is splashing up from the road and the windscreen wipers working at maximum speed testament to the poor driving conditions.

---

[24] 'Small is Beautiful', E E Schumacher (1973)

As the next sound erupts, a fight breaks out as the older sister can't take it anymore. "Just shut up" she yells, and then when told off for shouting in the car as I try to concentrate on getting us home safely "it's not fair, why am I the one who always get into trouble. She", pointing a finger at her little sister who is now pretending to be an angel, "started it".

There's no need to elaborate. We all know what family life can be like. Of course, it might not be a conventional 2.4 family but growing up and living with other people, often in close proximity, is a recipe for the odd fight. But there's also something very special about it.

Personally, I think 'Small [really is] beautiful". It in the smallness of our families and/or groups of friends that we can feel that we truly belong and care for others and be cared for. It is no coincidence that thousands of years after humans occupied the World, life is still organised around this small, special unit, and people, deprived of a secure childhood, whatever this looked like, often struggle long into adulthood with issues of self-worth and esteem.

I think it can be similar, albeit different, with small businesses, organisations or communities. In smallness, it is possible to know, value and build up relationships with people; to know what it really means to be human. Some years ago I moved from the suburbs of a city to a village. I had been worried that to truly belong would require decades of residence and that my status as an outsider would be a foregone conclusion. Thankfully my fears were unfounded and I found myself living in a community offering something I hadn't even realised was missing from my life. I'm not really even sure what I would call it; community spirit or a sense of being part of something bigger than myself? One of the most surprising things is how sometimes, inexplicably, a simple day to day interaction with a neighbour can lift my spirit. It's best put as the feeling that I am known which had been so alien in the rush of suburban life.

Of course, you don't need to live in a village to experience a sense of belonging. People find it in all kinds of ways, but it is true that our deepest needs are often met in entirely unexpected and entirely uneconomically-related ways. In contrast, in bigness, it's easy to find ourselves lonely in a roomful of people or answering on autopilot when people ask us 'how's it going'. They may mean well but I doubt they really care.

1973 saw the publication of Schumacher's "Small is Beautiful[25]" - a book formed of a collection of essays which for many remains unrivalled as the most persuasive and passionate critique of 'modern' economics in recent history. In it he challenges our understanding of, and relationship with, nature, arguing that Man sees himself as

---

[25] 'Small is Beautiful', E E Schumacher (1973)

'above it', his role to conquer and control it, rather than learn to live in harmony with it. Well ahead of the environmental movement today he understood that it was ludicrous to ignore the cost of the natural resources used to produce goods so loved by society, and the dangerous potential of unchecked economic growth.

Whilst not all of Schumacher's theories carry weight today, and his old-fashioned views about women would be enough to leave many reeling, he proved to have a remarkable insight about key World issues such as environmental destruction, pollution and urbanisation to name a few and was particularly concerned about the dangers of 'man' becoming no more than a cog in a machine.

I wonder what Schumacher would think were he alive today. It's true that many of the predictions he made of the future, were, if not entirely, mostly correct and I am sure he would feel a certain sense of satisfaction that his instincts were right. I doubt though, that this sense of satisfaction would last when he realised that his predictions of the damage inflicted on nature, were equally justified.

One thing I doubt he would have ever predicted is the level of technological change we have seen. The 1970s was the start of an era in many 'developed' countries which saw industry relocated to newly industrialised countries offering the prospect of lower wages and a chance for companies to save money. It coincided with a period of political change, and in the UK, the Thatcher years as the Government steered a course for the economy away from an era of making things with our hands, to an era of making money using our brains. It was a time of decline for massive industry as workers in steel and coal found themselves redundant and we are all familiar with the hardship that followed for many families.

Since then we have seen massive technological change far beyond the imagination of most people in the 1970s. When studying my degree in the 00s, I was tasked with researching the potential for smart phones to transform our lives. Even at that time just to send a text message meant working through each letter in the alphabet individually with the result that even a short message took ages to write. I recall the scepticism amongst my fellow students. Most, myself included, hypothesised that people would always use a desktop computer - who would choose a mobile phone? It was far beyond our imagination that today most people take their mobile phones everywhere and they serve as a primary source of entertainment, communication and organisation. In fact, we don't really need to go anywhere to survive today with the wide of apps on offer allowing us to shop from the comfort of our homes.

If Schumacher were alive today, I think he would be excited about the potential for these new technologies to transform markets. Far from treating 'man' as a cog in a machine, capabilities are such now that small, artisan designers and producers can sell their products to a wide market through internet technologies. I have brought bespoke, hand-made products from regions I have never visited through the wonders of such technology, at an attractive price compared to the 'big' option.

Yet, despite the ease with which we can now purchase items, we continue to live in a world dominated by bigness, and a World which values efficiency and profits above dignity and meaning, human life and nature.

I expect many of us could write essays about the mistreatment we have suffered at the hands of companies whom we suspect do not care enough about our business. We are meant to be won over by powerful advertising campaigns promising the World which in reality struggle to provide a back garden. I recall one experience of dealing with a big company. They crossed new boundaries in not caring. They wasted hours of my time and money, did not deliver the service they promised, and did not even have the decency to acknowledge my complaints; every communication I sent remains unanswered. It was perfectly clear that in their bigness, they simply did not care about 'little' me.

Even if we do like 'bigness' – and certainly there are industries where 'bigness' is essential - we have a problem if it dominates our World. The sheer size and power of some organisations today allows them to create and uphold inequality, placing power in the hands of a few. Worse, frequently these 'few' are not in office long enough to see out the consequence of their actions.

Recent years have seen more action from Shareholder Activists – people who attempt to use their rights as a shareholder of a publicly-traded corporation to bring about change within or for the corporation. Increasingly social and environmental issues dominate the agenda, with more people than ever before concerned about the way in which companies are governed.

These trends are encouraging and should drive positive change. However, I accept that many people will not feel they have the skills or the inclination to engage with this type of action. Many of the people I know outside my profession find it hard to understand the basics of investment, let alone how to engage companies on these issues. But we can make a decision about whether we like bigness, and what type of bigness we like.

Do we like bigness that cares for its employees over efficiency? Do we like bigness that puts its natural environment before profit? Do we like bigness that places animal welfare over cost? Do we like bigness that ensures everyone involved in delivering its goods and services is getting a fair share of the profits? Or do we support bigness for the sake of saving a few pounds?

Or would we prefer 'smallness'? Of course, it would be naïve to suggest that we return to the days of shopping separately for all our groceries. The ability to order all my shopping via an 'app' and have it all delivered to my home the next day is a life saver. Without it beans on toast would make a regular appearance for dinner as I would struggle to find time to keep the cupboards topped up. But we do need to consider the message we send to businesses. It is time we told companies across the World that we want companies who care; not just about their bottom line but about Society, their employees and their natural and living environments.

If we value life, we need creative companies to help make sure that as far as possible people involved in all aspects of supplying us with goods and services are getting a fair deal. The easy examples include tea, coffee, bananas and other fruit and vegetables where we now have well established 'fair trade' markets. It is hardly Rocket Science to write about fairly traded goods. Yet many of us chose other products leaving the destiny of thousands of suppliers to the whim of powerful global markets. Perhaps we are back to the familiar concept of penny pinching; maybe we do not like or feel we cannot afford the extra price tag that may be involved; or perhaps it is because we feel that fair trade products are not to our tastes; or maybe we are so stuck in our ways that it is unthinkable that we should depart from our favourite brands. Of course, making sure that people are getting a fair deal – particularly within developed countries – can get a bit tricky. And no-one wants their grocery shop to become horribly complicated.

In the early years of my marriage, it was a standing joke in our house that, talented chef that he is, my husband would cook Monday to Thursday and on Friday it was my turn. So, every Friday we would enjoy a takeaway from the local Chinese or stop for a curry on our way home from work, often following the traditional Friday night trip to the pub after work. When we became parents a limited budget mean that we would seek alternatives and soon my motto became that I would like something quick, tasty and easy. It remains so today. After all, who doesn't want an easy life?

It's a shame that it's not so easy to purchase sustainable products. I've often wondered why supermarkets are so poor at stocking alternatives to the household staples we've consumed for years. My eldest will soon reach adulthood yet when she was a baby, I had to source the biodegradable wipes I used online and would curse if I forgot and ended up with the nasty plastic variety. To my great delight for a short period of time my local supermarket did actually stock them before they disappeared from the shelves. Nearly 16 years later it's still the same. Similarly, I always source recycled toilet roll. Yet supermarkets offer few options and often I can only buy packs of 4 or they are out of stock. Shortly after the Covid-19 frenzied shopping spree I was delighted to see an entire shelf of recycled toilet rolls from a company claiming to "reflect the positive, the healthy and the sustainable[26]". These toilet rolls were made from fibers from a previous use and didn't use chorine or dyes. Yet, a few weeks later it was all being sold off because not enough people had bought it.

One of my favourite suppliers is a worker's co-operative, managed and owned by its workers. It strives to promote a more responsible lifestyle by supplying a wide range of ethical, ecological and socially responsible product lines. It's easy to find their products online, but you will rarely see them in the shops. What if you want to reduce your plastic waste? Instead of getting easier it seems to be getting harder to buy fruit and vegetables not encased in tonnes of plastic. I told myself on a recent shop that I would only buy non-packaged fresh produce – had I stuck to my principles I would have left with virtually nothing.

It would be easy to blame supermarkets for these failings but I suspect that we are all to blame. If there was a strong demand for these products, they would be flying off the shelves and supermarkets would be falling over themselves to sell them. One thing is sure, if the senior management of our big brands saw they were losing market share to sustainable alternatives they may actually make genuine changes to their products rather than trying to distract us with expensive advertising campaigns.

---

[26] https://www.myrenova.com/, Renova (2020)

If small really is beautiful, and sustainable is our future then we should seek out ways to build smallness into our everyday lives and support sustainable businesses and business practices. I work with many proprietors of small shops and service providers and know that the financial rewards are often questionable, particularly in light of the long hours often required to keep a business afloat. Yet during the Covid-19 pandemic, these businesses rallied around local communities, delivered groceries without charge to vulnerable people, kept their doors open when it would have been so easy to close them, and provided good value produce. We may not all be business leaders or have much influence on wider society, but we do all have a choice about where we shop, the types of businesses we support and the types of products we buy. We also have a choice about how we invest our money, such as the types of investments we purchase in our pensions.

However, we need to be careful not to create another brand of consumerism – a World of brand new sparkling electric cars boasting a socially conscious status and houses complete with the latest green technologies, bulging waste collection bins testament to the replacement of old products which were once our pride and joy. A World where only those with money have a voice.

And we must also be careful not to jump on a bandwagon without thinking it through. I wrote earlier how I gave up meat in my diet. People are often confused when I explain I still eat fish and dairy and in fact, don't really object to eating meat. I just think we should eat less of it, and for me, that meant giving it up completely. Today, Veganism has become trendy and many people now identify as such. Consequently, it's now possible to purchase Vegan options with relative ease. Vegan values present much to be admired, with its early beliefs such as avoiding exploitation and cruelty to animals now expanded into a wider concern for the environment. But I wonder what people who have followed a Vegan diet for many years feel about today's commercialisation of their beliefs. As a Pescatarian I have never been tempted to eat fake versions of traditional meat products such as bacon, and rarely eat processed vegetarian options, preferring to eat fresh vegetables and pulses. Yet today Supermarket shelves are bursting with such products, all 'nicely' encased in plastic and mass produced in energy hungry factories.

Reworking our relationship with money will be perhaps our most challenging task to achieve meaningful change in our lives. Instead of seeing it as something to be hoarded and used to get as much as we possibly can for ourselves, we need to create a culture where money is a means to distribute the World's resources so that everyone has the chance to live.

It will be hard because money is a very emotive subject. We love it. We hate it. We delight in it. We fight about it. We worry about not having enough. We worry about losing what we have. We are generous with it. We are stingy with it. We use it to bring us Joy. We get angry about it. And financial regulators are fixated with the risk of us losing it.

Perhaps many of us allow money to have too much influence over our lives and happiness. A friend of mine was recounting how angry he was that he had received a letter which had not been franked. As the tale unraveled, I expected him to describe how this simple mistake cost an exorbitant amount of money or how hours of his time were wasted in a bid to secure its release - such was his rage. But no, it transpired that the whole episode cost little more than a pound and a three-mile trip in the car.

If we are honest, we all get too angry at times about silly unimportant things. I used to get angry wasting money on fines, particularly credit card fines; less than twenty-four hours late and immediately you accrue hefty charges and extra interest. My bank used to allow one day's grace for outstanding payments – this propelled them several rungs up the ladder in my opinion. Now the payment date has been brought forward and there is no such leniency.

Whilst many of us waste our time with this type of anger we do not get angry about the things we should. We do not get angry that places of beauty are being destroyed in the pursuit of material pleasure. We do not get angry that millions of people are being mistreated and millions others are needlessly dying each year. But we should get angry about these things.

And perhaps we are too stingy. We put a pound or two in the odd collection bucket or may even donate money and clothing to our favourite charity. We think we are being generous. The truth is that often we are not. I wonder how many charity shops receive clothing far beyond reuse whilst we hold onto better quality items in the hope that they will still fit us when they come back into fashion.

As we emerge from the global chaos of the Coronavirus pandemic and study its impact on our lives and economies, we have been given a unique opportunity to change. Politicians around the World are now considering how to stimulate economic growth with some countries announcing infrastructure projects on a scale not seen for decades as other forms of economic stimulus, principally interest rates, have become dead ducks killed by years of being kept artificially low.

So, we have a choice, we can pursue these projects treating the Earth and nature as something to 'conquer and control' or we can respect it, understanding that to do anything else would be derisible. As with no planet we have no future.

We need to understand that our money and the public purse, should be used to pursue the greenest options, to invest in projects which are sustainable and put us in a place of security for our future and that of our children and grandchildren. Naturally, there will always be compromise, a balance should be sought, but to continue to treat the Earth as ours to plunder – a free resource – would be the biggest mistake we could ever make.

It may be coincidence that in the UK we were blessed with beautiful weather over the first 'lockdown'. But during that time there was a part of me that liked to think of it as nature smiling back at us as it enjoyed a brief reprieve from our usual bad habits.

CHAPTER 11

THE END OR THE BEGINNING

"It's the final countdown..de na na na..."

You probably know the song. What we don't know is how long the countdown will be; how long until our relentless pursuit for growth in the name of 'progress' takes an overwhelming toll on our Society, our lives and our planet.

Sometimes I wonder what we must look like to observers from space; the ever increasing expanse of industry; the growing sprawl of urbanization; the unsightly slums sitting innocently alongside luxury resorts; the destruction of countryside and forests; the places submerged in water and the places scorched with heat; and on closer inspection the millions of people rushing around on parts of the planet losing their health in a failing quest for happiness whilst in other places people are dying from poverty without the strength to work.

I truly believe that we need a more creative type of economic growth; growth which does not literally cost us the Earth and rob thousands of people of their health and many, many more of even the chance to live. We need life-giving economics, and importantly, we need Governments, men and women who agree; men and women who believe that together we can change the World.

I have argued that creative economics starts with ourselves and understanding what is really important to us; what we really want people to say about us when our lives are over; what we really value. If we are to be creative, we need to make sure we respect our values when we decide what goods and services we buy and who we buy them from. Consumption does not have to be destructive; we can make it creative.

Perhaps the biggest challenge we face is giving up our love affair with money. We must forget about hoarding as much money as possible for ourselves with little thought for the consequences. Instead we must once again return to the idea of money as a means of exchange and make sure that when we are exchanging money for goods and services, we are exchanging a fair amount of money for creative goods and services and that we are investing it in industries and companies which care. Money's greatest flaw – that it tells us only the price of something and not the cost to our Society and World – is also Man's greatest weakness.

Instead, let's imagine a World, fueled not by how much we can have or how much we can consume but by how much we can live creatively and how much that creativity can bless others. Imagine a Natural World where plants and species are not being destroyed in the name of progress but a Natural World where nature knows no abounds and we are continuously astonished by its beauty. Imagine a Living World not fighting to survive man's deadly touch as one by one other species die out but a Living World bursting with life. Imagine a Living World not locked in cages and subjected to terrible living conditions but a Living World given the chance to enjoy its sometimes-fleeting opportunity to live. Imagine a Corporate World obsessed not with making short term profits at any cost but a Corporate World creatively making profits without compromising our society, equality, or our natural and living environment.

This type of world means the end of working without any idea of what we really want to achieve and instead working out our ambitions and dreams. It means the end of treating employees like parts of a machine and the beginning of recognizing their humanity and their creativity. It means the end of wasting money on 'useless' tack and silly gadgets, and it means the beginning of creative products and enriching services. It means the end of poor-quality sofas and dodgy fridge freezers and the rebirth of lifetime guarantees. It means the end of wasteful habits and disposable packaging, and a return to wartime ingenuity and creative recycling. It means the end of exploitatively cheap goods and the beginning of life for millions of people. It means change. And this change will not be easy, but it has the potential to be very, very worthwhile.

My final plea is simple, the World needs creative consumers, creative employers and creative companies and we need them now. It is time we refuse to accept the status quo. It is time we refused to "go with the flow". It is time we do not accept things as they are and did something about them. It is time we are willing to do something to end poverty. It is time we are willing to do something to reduce disease. It is time we do something to have better, deeper relationships with our friends and family. It is time we do something to contribute to a fairer Society. It is time we do something to build trust in our community. And it is time we realise that these things are attainable.

We need to remember that we have a capacity for change and to change things around us. We need to remember that we can creatively make the rules and systems we live by work a little better for our World. Crucially we need to have the courage to become creative consumers.

Finally, I accept that there are some people who will dismiss my words as those of an idealistic dreamer. Even if this is your opinion, I do have one small request, please...no more tack for Christmas!

ABOUT THE AUTHOR

Holly Heald is a Wife, Mother to three daughters, business leader and Chartered Financial Planner living and working in Norfolk, UK. She is passionate about the difference that good business can make to people's lives and the positive role it can play in our futures. In her spare time she enjoys spending time with her family and friends, reading, music, keeping fit, good food and great wine.

Lightning Source UK Ltd.
Milton Keynes UK
UKHW021824031022
409847UK00011B/2819